Mirror of the Free

First published by O-Books, 2011
O-Books is an imprint of John Hunt Publishing Ltd., Laurel House, Station Approach,
Alresford, Hants, SO24 9JH, UK
office1@o-books.net
www.o-books.com

For distributor details and how to order please visit the 'Ordering' section on our website.

ISBN: 978 1 84694 419 2

A CIP catalogue record for this book is available from the British Library.

Design: Stuart Davies

Printed in the UK by CPI Antony Rowe
Printed in the USA by Offset Paperback Mfrs, Inc

We operate a distinctive and ethical publishing philosophy in all
areas of our business, from our global network of authors to
production and worldwide distribution.

Mirror of the Free

Nicholas Swift

BOOKS

Winchester, UK
Washington, USA

Mirror of the Free

It is common for authors of books on the Tarot cards to assert that their true origin is unknown. One sometimes gets the impression, however, that they prefer it that way: knowledge means not only less excuse to speculate but, also, more responsibility. They write as if they want to know; or as if they want the reader to think they want to; or as if acknowledging, almost reluctantly, that they ought to make an earnest effort to find out: but, when it comes down to it, they might, for some reason, really rather not.

The situation is in some ways reminiscent of the multiplicity of points of view about other historical mysteries. In the case, for instance, of the opening of King Tutankhamen's tomb, there was the matter of the supposed curse. Superstitious subsequent explorers find themselves wondering whether anything bad will happen if they violate this or that holy mystery.

A less glamorous and more realistic threat, however, is that of a sense of anticlimax. It could happen that instead of enjoying the mystery, one finds one has to work at understanding something.

It is true that if you read this book you may find it difficult to continue to justify the uses to which you are accustomed to putting the Tarot: not necessarily because you are disappointed by the new information, but because you decide that there is a great deal more to the Tarot than you ever suspected; having become aware of certain facts, which may conflict with your beliefs, you may feel that you have to shed some of them.

If what you are already doing with the cards, as they say, 'works for you,' you may even find that what is offered here constitutes an opportunity to come to a deeper understanding of what it is you have really been doing all along: that the numinosity has brightened, not dimmed.

Favorite theories include that the images are from ancient Egypt, and represent stages of some sort of initiation, and were shown on walls past which the initiate into esoteric mysteries had to go; that they were compiled by the priests of such mysteries, and later rendered a humble deck of cards precisely for the sake of preserving them, using a hiding-in-plain-sight strategy; that they came from India; that they have something to do with gypsies, who have made them a part of their nomadic culture, and are especially skilled at their divinatory use; that they never were anything more than a game; that they contain all the secrets of creation; that the widely accepted form and the order of the cards are somehow incorrect; that they are somehow connected with the Kabbalah (or Cabala, or Qabalah), and perhaps with ritual magic; that they express truths only accessible by means of man's own unconscious mind, collective or otherwise, and that, as such, they may be said to correspond to archetypes; and so on.

The pages to follow show that while there is some truth in some of these beliefs, when they are right, they are usually distorted. They also overlook some of the most important facts about the Tarot.

One thing appears certain, however: it was never just a game. Those who insist that it always was and is no more than that are probably people who need it to be that way for reasons of their own.

The few available real clues, then, point in directions inconsistent with most of the received wisdom about the Tarot. It may then incorrectly be assumed that the darkness the trail disappears into must be forever impenetrable; that it is the darkness of secrets that are real secrets, and that have been held and continue to be held by the people who hold them; and, that being the case, the only hope is to be told what they are by those people.

Can it be even that simple, though? Apparently not. Attempts to identify those people lead to the discovery that the Tarot may be one of many artifacts of their previous and perhaps current activity, and that they may even expect some struggle in the efforts to learn from it, without and before hands being thrown up and defeat admitted.

It may be that simply being told something, especially something important, is not enough if it is going to sink in and be valued as it deserves.

Perhaps one of the things to be developed out of that struggle is the ability to identify other people, ones who have gone to the other extreme – and they may greatly outnumber the ones who are able to acknowledge that there is a point beyond which they cannot be their own teachers – and have manufactured systems they present as conclusive, based on the fragments they have pieced together, whether of the Tarot alone or in combination with other phenomena: which does not mean that such syncretistic systems are altogether without interest, because it could be that their manufacture, as incomplete and distorted and of-their-time as they are, was not only anticipated, but counted on by the keepers of the real secrets, the real knowledge: precisely because there has to be a beginning, and so that learning can take place by degrees.

The question arises of the 'proper order' for the cards.

If it is our argument (and it is) that the Tarot as we know it is a distorted, partial, accreted-upon, and mistranslated thing, then it stands to reason that the order popularly imposed on it is equally untrustworthy.

There is no correct order to the Tarot cards.

If the levels of meaning concealed by the Tarot turn out to include something that could be called sequentiality, and those levels of meaning can only be discovered by referring to quite other materials, then that sequentiality, to whatever it may pertain, can, obviously, have nothing meaningful to do with the superficial order of the cards themselves.

Once more, then, to be sure: there is no particular order to the Tarot and, in view of the admission of ignorance that has to be the starting point of any significant study of them, there is no other aspect of them, either, that dictates a necessary or preferred order in which to pursue that study. Almost all books on the Tarot start with The Magician, because it is the first card in the pack. (Others say it should be The Fool.)

If, however, the Magician is truly a magician, what need would he have of such a study?

On the other hand, if the Fool really is such a fool, what would he want with it?

Transformation, as any tactful or simply worried Tarot card reader will say, is the real meaning of...

Figure 1. Tarot. Death.

An old Laurel and Hardy film had an ending likely to be experienced as horrific by any child, such as may be expected to have watched it. The buffoonish duo had lost their bodies from the head down, except for the bones: yet they were still alive. Animated skeletons, they walked, Ollie with his characteristic irritated expression, and Stan grimacing and lachrymose, for once with good reason.

'Here's another fine mess you've gotten me into!' snapped Oliver, as usual.

Looking at the Marseille Tarot, a particular design the earliest surviving examples of which are debated as dating from the sixteenth century, and which is so called because of its association, since the early part of the twentieth century, with Marseille, France (although there are literary references from fourteenth century Marseille that have been interpreted as references to cards), we may be forgiven for thinking that someone has got us into a fine mess with it; even while we feel we can understand the churning horror that the image of the Grim Reaper must have aroused among Europeans of those plague-infested times.

While the very earliest decks that have survived are differently styled, it is a logical implication of the theory of the Tarot's origins being presented here that other Tarot decks were very likely derived from the Marseille Tarot. The reasons for thinking so will become evident. The innovations in the other decks appear to have been products of the imagination of artists elaborating on the basic Marseille design, whether or not they have attempted to justify their changes by reference to a wide variety of theories involving symbolism.

While the Marseille images themselves, even when skillfully executed, have a capacity to evoke a spectrum of responses that include a sense of unease, even of the sinister, probably attributable to what amounts to their ambiguity (circumventing the habit of the mind to instantly classify and, thus, dismiss), there is, in most examples, another ambiguity, which is a cruder one, and results from the fact that the figures are not, frankly, drawn very well. Limbs are out of place, perspectives are askew, lots of bits of things are there that don't really seem to fit or make much sense: and, more often than not, it even looks as if the artist has tried to *make it* make sense, with the results that we see.

That, it is now apparent, is because he didn't know the sense it was supposed to make.

Figure 1 is the Death card as it appears, with minor variations, in a large number of Marseille or Marseille-based Tarots.

The skull does not, particularly, look like a skull. It resembles, perhaps, the emaciated face of someone who, in addition to being emaciated, is suffering from some dental affliction, and has a cloth wrapped around his head. The rest of the figure is a garbled rendition of a human skeleton; or, if one wants to be generous, a deteriorated but animated corpse: that way it doesn't have to be all that accurate anatomically, because who knows what that would look like anyway, with scraps of flesh sticking randomly like mud in a scandal?

Death, of course, wields a sickle, with which it cuts down all things. One foot is on the removed head of a woman, and another head is in the other corner. Hands and a foot lie among the flora.

As anyone knows who has explored the cards for their use along the lines of divination – or, less ambitiously, evocation of an intuitive response – colors matter a great deal, as they do in every area of life where atmosphere is a concern. Vividness and bleakness, too, can each have a significance in its own right.

What you think the Tarot card Death means will unavoidably owe something to what you think death itself is. Seeing it as annihilation, with no continuation of consciousness or spirit, no soul, no other realities in and on to which the human essence goes to pursue its destinies, is unlikely to be consistent with being open to the notion of non-obvious meanings, and more likely to accompany seeing the Tarot as only a game.

Every end, it goes or should go without saying, is also a beginning and, invariably, this truth is taken into account by those who write about the Tarot when it comes to this card. (Apart from anything else, it would not go down very well with Miss Dimplebottom to tell her that the bulge in the pocket of the tall dark and handsome stranger she is going to meet is a sharp farming implement.)

Transformation is obviously something that is always occurring, on many levels and in many departments of life, including that of the individual. One is doing no more – and no less – than quoting mystics of all times and places to say that death means transformation. When the image comes up, if the topic of discussion is the Tarot as used for divination or counseling, it then becomes a matter of identifying the thing facing transformation.

As filmmakers like Ingmar Bergman knew – and one of his admirers is Woody Allen, whose character in his 1975 comedy *Love and Death* famously said, 'I don't want to achieve immortality through my work; I want to achieve immortality by not dying' – the use of black and white opens up possibilities harder to achieve with color. Colors can, as it were, get in the way. Focusing on a more limited range of impressions – in this case, black and white and the shades of grey in between – allows for greater concentration on the nuances; in other words, subtlety. In some wisdom traditions, the term 'subtlety' is even applied to a different range of perceptions, considered by some metaphysical or spiritual.

Figure 2. Detail of cylinder seal from Tello (Girsu), Mesopotamia; Akkad period, 2330–2150 BCE. Louvre, Paris.

Looking at photographs of impressions made by Mesopotamian cylinder seals can be almost like looking at an old – a *very* old – black-and-white photograph.

Because they are physically relatively shallow impressions, and have to be highlighted to be clearly discerned, the seals have an eeriness about them, attributable though this may be to our conditioning through occupying the place we do in the history of visual media. (The present book uses charcoal pencil drawings closely based on the originals.)

Figure 2 shows a Mesopotamian deity that has not been identified with certainty.

How do we know it is a god? By the horns. Its head-gear, if you look closely, is curled up at each side. In the times and at the place, one of the ways that gods and goddesses were recognized was by their horns.

Isn't that the wrong way round, though? Isn't it the Devil who has horns?

If it is a god – and thus corresponds, presumably, to something good – *why* does it have horns?

Or is it just proof that all those old pagans were wicked anyway, worshipping what we now know to have been evil?

The subject of evil – whether it may be said to really exist (if God is good, how can it?), or whether it is, rather, only the absence of good (if, again, God is all powerful, how is that possible?) – is obviously one of the conundrums the answer to which may only come with the attaining of real wisdom, and there may be as many answers to it as there are levels of the latter. It may even be an inspiration to seek it. Recall the story of how finding out that the world was not all good compelled Prince Siddhartha to leave his life of oblivious comfort and set out on the path that culminated in his becoming the Buddha.

On a more basic cultural and, even, psychological level, the issue of the Devil being, in popular imagination, a creature with horns relates critically to the question of the difference between appearance and reality.

The same theme features in a brief passage in *Ihya 'Alam ad Din* (*Revival of Religious Knowledge*) by the exceedingly influential eleventh (CE) century Muslim thinker and Sufi Abu Hamid al Ghazali.

In discussing knowledge of 'the world' and contrasting it with that of spiritual things, he wrote: 'He who is experienced in the religious sciences is inexperienced in worldly learning. For this reason, the Prophet said: 'Most of the inmates of Paradise are indifferent': in other words, they are inattentive to worldly matters.'

It is the next line, however, that is arresting in the context of considering understanding of 'devils' or 'the Devil,' mainly

8

because the way in which it is phrased would seem to suggest that it might allude to the reported ability of Sufi masters to somehow experience the immediate, living presence of other Sufis of the past and future, even the distant past and future, and to communicate with them: Ghazali quotes another historically prominent Sufi named Hasan al Basri ('of Basra'), thus:

'We have seen such people whom you would think, if you had seen them, diabolical...If they had seen you, however, they would call you devils.'

Basra was, at the time of Hasan – and is still today – in what is now called Iraq. Indeed, it is only a few miles from the modern city Babylon.

'*They* would call *you* devils...'

Who were the Mesopotamians, and what are their cylinder seals?

'Meso-' means 'between,' and 'Mesopotamia' refers to the area between the Tigris and Euphrates rivers. In its common use of 'ancient Mesopotamia,' however, it applies more broadly to the societies that flourished there and somewhat further afield from the time of the Sumerians, whose origins both racially and culturally remain unknown, through periods of the inhabitants' conquest – peaceful or, more often, violent – by other peoples. Only recent archeological discoveries elsewhere in the Middle East (Hamoukar, in Syria, was a large and highly developed city at least contemporaneous with Sumer, and the village of Catal Huyuk, in what is now Anatolia, Turkey, antedates both) have removed the Sumerians from the exclusive position they long held as the first known civilization. They were not themselves Semites, but were conquered, over the course of centuries, by the Amorites, who *were* Semites, as were the Elamites, the Akkadians, the Aramaeans (or Chaldeans), the Hittites, and others, and then the Assyrians, who were themselves eventually conquered by the Persians, who were... Persian.

Ur, Babylon, Babel and Nineveh are among the names of great

cities in this region that may evoke memories of Sunday school or Torah class, assuming that the reader has managed in the time since to loosen the grip on his or her imagination of the compelling document known (to nominal Christians, anyway) as the Old Testament as he blossomed into adulthood.

(It continues to be a source of perplexity to some how many others who consider themselves highly qualified *aficionados* of 'Judeo-Christianity' have no conception of the degree to which their beliefs derive from the other, earlier civilizations of the region in question, assuming that they are even aware of their beliefs' history, which many of them are not. The stories of the Flood and of the Tower of Babel, and much else, were told among members of the Mesopotamian cultures long before Abram-to-be-Abraham came out of 'Ur of the Chaldees'; and the work of modern researchers, such as Israel Finkelstein and Neil Asher Silberman, in *The Bible Unearthed*, liberates the student from any obligation he might have felt to consider the stories historically accurate.)

While history was history even then, though, and political and racial hegemonies were inconstant, what did persist was the pantheon of gods and goddesses. Although their names varied, and different sacred stories, or myths, as they are also called, were told about them in different places within the area, they, the deities themselves, can sometimes even be seen as blending into each other. When the Kassites, for example, from the north east, took over, they did so peacefully, and made the extant culture and religion their own.

Religion persisted even when political change was tumultuous; and, even where a Sumerian antecedent for a given Babylonian myth is yet undiscovered, the current scholarly consensus is that it probably existed.

Mesopotamian mythology is, therefore, Sumerian mythology; in the south, both the Akkadians and, later, the Amorites, both Semitic peoples, adopted it. So did the Assyrians in the north, until, around 612 BCE, their empire and their capital, Nineveh, were conquered by the Medes and Nabopolassar of Babylon. The same mythology and religion then persisted under the Babylonian kings, right through the rise to power of the Aramaeans, or Chaldeans, from the western plains, and under their rule until Cyrus the Great of Persia took Babylon in 538 BCE, bringing with him Zoroastrianism, which itself owed much to Babylonian astronomy (yet is considered by some to be a form of monotheism), and which, through the implementation of the policies of Cyrus the Great, in turn shaped, in many ways, the thoughts of Jewish philosophers of later centuries, especially with regard to the concept of the messiah. The names of the angels in the Hebrew scriptures, for instance, derive from the teachings of Zar-tusht, or Zoroaster.

What about the cylinder seals, then?

Describing their physical characteristics and mode of manufacture, and some of the uses to which they were put, is much easier than identifying the significance of the images they preserve. Usually made of stone, although sometimes of other substances, such as shell, they are, as their name indicates, cylindrical, and they have a hole through the axis, presumably for ease of application or preservation, or both. Finely carved on them are designs that, when the cylinder is rolled on soft clay, are impressed on it, thereby creating images in relief. Although large quantities of cylinder seals have been recovered, the work of understanding the import of the pictures they convey is very far from complete. It is known that the seals were used in official and formal contexts, such as enshrining agreements and marking property, as well as in apparently decorative ones.

Why are they of interest in relation to the Tarot?

A comparison of Figure 1 with Figure 2 may constitute some small preparation for what Helena ('Madame') Blavatsky, founder of the well known Theosophical Society, and author of many books on occult subjects, had to say about it, not in any of the volumes for which she is famous but, rather, in her correspondence:

'Again the Alphabet of Thoth can be dimly traced in the modern Tarot which can be had at almost every bookseller's in Paris. As for its being understood or utilized, the many fortune-tellers in Paris, who make a professional living by it, are sad specimens of failures of attempts at reading, let alone correctly interpreting, the symbolism of the Tarot without a preliminary philosophical study of the Science. The real Tarot, in its complete symbology, can be found only in the Babylonian cylinders, that anyone can inspect and study in the British Museum and elsewhere. Anyone can see these Chaldean, antediluvian rhombs, or revolving cylinders, covered with sacred signs; but the secrets of these divining 'wheels,' or, as de Mirville calls them, 'the rotating globes of Hecate,' have to be left untold for some time to come. Meanwhile there are the 'turning-tables' of the modern medium for the babes, and the Kabbalah for the strong. This may afford some consolation.'[1]

Elsewhere she says:

'There are two taros – the wheel purely Esoteric, and the Western tarot – Kabalistical, remodelled by Shemites, a branch so much younger than the Aryans and even the Hamites. The latter taro (tarot) is to be read from right to left like Arabic and Hebrew writing. The former, primitive 'Wheel' is in Cuneiform characters and astrological signs.'[2]

Cuneiform is the name given to the form of writing of the Mesopotamians, consisting of angular impressions in clay. An enormous amount of the cuneiform material recovered by archaeologists remains untranslated.

In yet a third place, she asserted still further connections:

'This makes it plain that the Kabalah of the Jews is but the distorted echo of the Secret Doctrine of the Chaldeans, and that the real Kabalah is found only in the Chaldean Book of Numbers now in the possession of some Persian Sufis.'[3]

The individual – or god, if you like – shown in Figure 2 is doing something with something. (Unfortunately, it sometimes really is hardly possible to say any more than that about what is going on in these seals. In addition, one needs to beware of experts whose ruling principle seems to be, 'When in doubt, say it's a fertility ritual.') He appears to be holding down something that looks like it could be a branch, if those things clustered along it are smaller branches with leaves, using one foot and his left hand, and using his right hand to chop away at it with a tool.

No further light is instantly shed on his intentions by the addition of the rest of the scene (Figure 3). Under the bent branch someone is crouching, identifiable as female by her long hair. The horns, again, mark her as a deity, as they do the individual holding a mace or similar object and popping, apparently, out from (behind?) the lower trunk of the tree like

Figure 3. Cylinder seal of unidentified deities. Tello.

a character in a Warner Brothers cartoon. A plausible assumption is that it is a scene from a myth, but which myth and which gods are yet unknown.

It has been speculated that the latter two figures are, respectively, the extremely important female deity known as Inanna to the Sumerians and to subsequent Semitic peoples as Ishtar, the goddess of sexual love and of war, who was yet also sometimes a 'Mother Goddess,' and the shepherd who, in one myth, was her lover, Dumuzi or Tammuz. One myth tells how she chose Dumuzi for her husband over Enkimdu the farmer, after Enkimdu and Dumuzi had an argument in which Dumuzi asserted the greater profitability of his flocks and herds, and that culminated in Enkimdu agreeing to let Dumuzi graze his flocks on his land. There may be an intersection here with the story in Genesis of Cain and Abel: the animal sacrifice of Abel, the herdsman, was accepted where the vegetable one of Cain was not. Like Abel, Dumuzi ended up dead, although only part time, and not by the hand of his former rival.

The most important myth, however, about Inanna/Ishtar and Dumuzi/Tammuz is the one about her descent into the underworld. Although her reasons for going are not entirely clear, before she left, she told Ninshubur, her vizier, or second-in-command, that if she did not come back, he should go and call on the three greatest gods, Enlil, Nanna, and Enki, for help. She had to pass through seven gates, and remove an article of clothing or jewelry at each one; so that, by the time she reached the bottom, she was naked and utterly vulnerable. Ereshkigal, the ruler of the underworld, was her own sister; once in her presence, Ishtar attempted to seize her throne, but failed; and, as punishment, she was sentenced to death, and her corpse hung from a nail. Ninshubur, surmising the worst, did as he had been told. The god of wisdom, Enki, created two creatures from the dirt under his fingernails, and gave them, respectively, the Plant of Life and the

Water of Life. Revisiting Ishtar with them sixty times, they revived her.

The arrangement arrived at for her departure and return to the land of the living was that she provide a substitute for herself. In a move many ex-husbands will find all too familiar, she chose Dumuzi, and left in the company of horrible demons. Dumuzi was required to spend half of the year in the underworld, and his sister the other half.

Figure 4. Detail of cylinder seal.

No one knows for certain that the characters shown in Figure 3 are Inanna and Dumuzi, with Enkimdu on the left dancing a jig on seeing the way things turned out.

Let us now look at the crouching female figure – the fact that these individuals sport *multiple* horns indicates that they are not your common-or-garden deities (vegetation and fertility and so on notwithstanding), but high-ranking gods – isolated in Figure 4 and, next to her, the Star card from the Tarot.

Typical meanings within the context of a divinatory spread for this card, as supplied by manufacturers, include things like 'faith,' 'inspiration,' 'bright future,' and

Figure 5. Tarot. The Star.

also, 'mixing together of present and past.' In the reversed position, logically, it is taken to indicate 'loss of opportunities,' among other things.

It is not difficult to see how positive interpretations suggest themselves when looking at The Star. ('How can you go wrong,' many would say, 'with a naked woman?') On top of that, she looks, if not necessarily very young – although she may be – not old.

If the name of the card is to be taken into consideration in trying to come to some understanding of it – and it can hardly not be; although the significance of the names relative to the images is great, it is not necessarily in the way one might expect, as will be discussed later – it can be inferred only that the woman is meant to be thought of as some kind of star, since she is obviously the central image, and the name is 'The Star,' and not 'The Stars.' She is performing this mysterious act of pouring, apparently water, from two vessels. Many have taken it that she is pouring from one vessel onto the dry ground and, from the other, into what is evidently a river or other body of water.

The figure's femininity and nudity suggest a delicacy and

vulnerability consistent with a status in turn suggestive of a non-terrestrial or sublime nature, and her activity looks like some form of nurturing: a transmission of some sort of vitality or energy from a higher level to a lower one; and the fact that she is doing it at night suggests secrecy or, at least, the unseen.

Another reasonable assumption is that it is night, because stars are invisible in the day. A delicate and more refined reality, a 'higher' reality, an active reality, a reality not ordinarily perceptible by us in our sun-illuminated world of blunt contrasts and loud colors and near objects – nearer, by far, than the stars: and she – in traditional, or old fashioned, thinking, the passive gender – is engaged in an odd, secretive activity: she adds water to water with one hand and, with the other, pours it on the dry earth.

Assuming, too, that the water she pours is representative of an influence, to be no more specific, from her own sublime level, what may be inferred from the fact that there is (taking into account the detail referred to) already water there, to which she is adding it?

If the earth on which she kneels is our earth, then the water that is already there must be those things already in our world that have some relationship with worlds 'above.' Of course, it will be impossible for some to accept that there is anything of that nature. Civilization itself, perhaps, or the best part of civilization – depending on what you believe about what civilization is, and where it comes from, and its purpose – may be what is meant. If the purpose of civilization is to enable mankind to rise above itself, then this part of the message of the card would seem to be that the link with the source is an active one, a conscious one: a living, intelligent being is engaging in a deliberate act.

If the earth – as distinct from the water on the earth in the image – represents, in fact, 'the Earth' – in other words, the material planet and foundation for that which is built upon it, then the implication, proceeding from the significance of the water poured into the water, would seem to be that the continued existence of it, too, somehow depends on this nurturing of a cosmic and rarefied, if still mostly obscure, nature. This, surely, is less expected.

Taking the water-already-on-the-ground as representing civilization, if not in the broadest sense, then in the sense of whatever it is that makes civilizations come into, and stay in, existence, it may be worth considering whether the figure of the girl and her activity are references to what some authors, such as the late J. G. Bennett, following the lead of Gurdjieff, who followed the lead of Sufis, have maintained is a kind of evolutionary force among humanity, called by such names as the title of one of Bennett's books (*The Masters of Wisdom*).

Along similar lines are the claims that religions – and, even, human biological evolution itself— are also products of intervention by intelligences not native to our planet. Since the Sufis also claim to have originated the religions of history, the possibility of an intriguing resonance is raised.

On a level at once more elementary and more transcendent – in other words, closer to the source – is the question of the implications for this scenario in a way that, as it were, precedes sociology.

Books containing selections from Rumi's poetry have become very popular, although, seeing the way in which they are evidently intended to be used, one cannot help wondering how close that use is to Rumi's intention.

However that may be, in *Fihi Ma Fihi* (*What is in it is in it*), a record of his spoken teaching, Rumi is quoted as saying:

'This world is kept in existence by a finer reality. To you it is real because you can see and feel it, and the realities of which this world is only a branch seem to you imaginary. It is actually the other way around. It is this world that is imaginary. Higher truth produces innumerable worlds just like it, and they all decay and disappear; it then produces a new and better one, while itself never decaying, being beyond 'new' and 'old.''

In Sufi metaphysics – at least, as formulated within the Islamic religious framework – worlds of increasing coarseness emanate from an ultimately unknowable absolute. The nature of that absolute, and of the relatively real worlds, and of the relationship between these, are the subjects of much of its literature.

The authors of such works sometimes speak of one reality 'flowing' into another, lower one or, even, 'overflowing,' this overflow then itself constituting the next one, so emphasizing the independence of the former from the latter and, by implication, its superiority to it. Another aspect of the relationship is that the higher level is active in relation to the one below it, which is thus passive to the higher one; but that one is, in turn, active in relation to the next one below it, until you get to our world, the ability of the denizens of which to perceive such causal interrelationships few would claim is universally enhanced by their enjoying that status, as demonstrated by the tendency, for instance, to put batteries in the wrong way round.

An important part of this scheme is the role of what in Islamic Sufism are called the Names of God, which are, to put it concisely, the source of everything in creation, inasmuch as they are the ultimate realities of all qualities.

Shah Waliullah of Delhi, a major eighteenth century Sufi and philosopher, wrote that 'the substance and the secret of a thing is that aspect of the patient' (that is, the passive) 'which is present in its agent' (that is, the active) '(and has become the cause of its creation).'[4] In other words, the innermost essence, the real nature, of anything is not to be discovered by considering the thing in the context of its appearance, of its existence among all the other things in what we think of as the world, but, rather, in a higher level of reality altogether, the level in which that thing has its real origin.

Not only our poor planet Earth, but the whole of the universe we are capable of perceiving with our ordinary eyes, Waliullah says, 'is under the force of Will (and) originates in the mingled-up predications of the Names (of God). There' (in our ordinary world) 'the predications of the Names are so mingled up that the whole of one thing is hardly to be found in perfect agreement with the whole of any other thing.'[5]

The duality of the water-giving vessels in the Star girl's hands suggests a significant dichotomy. The theme of duality itself can constitute something of a thread through the study of the subject, but one of the most important dualities in this context that echoes the sameness of the water as source and water as receptacle on the one hand, and water as source only on the other (and thus, indeed, the whole, large theme of sameness-versus-difference), is that of Mercy and Power.

Waliullah says that the first name of God is 'Allah'; below it come the names of 'the first, the greatest, the noblest and the simplest emanation,' namely, 'The Living, the Self-Subsistent, the Real, the Light.' From 'the Self-Subsistent' come 'the Glorious, the Magnificent, the Most High, the Great, the Exalted.' From 'the Great' come 'the Independent, the Comprehensive, the Strong, the Overcoming, the Blessed,' and from 'the Blessed' come 'the Munificent, the Merciful, the Just, the Powerful.'[6]

'Mercy and Power,' Waliullah tells us, 'are an exposition of one of the aspects of the Blessed. It is an aspect which has the capability for all the overflowing perfections which are represented in the form of a faculty for it, but it is devoid of an actual overflow. This aspect is self-spreading by essence.

'Mercy and Power,' he continues, 'are the same thing. The possession of power over everything is the sign of His mercy...What is beyond that (representation of mercy) is named as power...Thereafter, when Mercy appeared in the form of an actual overflow it was named as Will. It is as an aspect of unity, and is as if a seal of musk for infinity and absoluteness.'

Then, almost as if looking over our shoulder as we contemplate the female figure in the card, he adds: 'No ambitious mind has any right to look for anything else primarily and essentially.'[7]

Mercy and Power, that is, are the same thing (the water), yet there are these two aspects to it (the two vessels). The thing of which Mercy and Power are aspects does not itself overflow, yet it contains, somehow, within itself all the further overflowings ('overflowing perfections') that may ensue. In whatever realm it is in which Mercy seems to have some sort of limit, beyond which what was previously experienced as Mercy is experienced as Power, Mercy may yet overflow, and if and when it does, it does so as a manifestation of Will (God's will, presumably; yet bear in mind that Waliullah has already said that the thing of which Mercy and Power are aspects is, in itself, an 'essence': another theme to be taken up later).

Can the act portrayed in the Star card be construed as a representation of the action of this Will? Mercy poured on that which can receive it, and beyond that there ought only to be Power – yet she still pours the waters of Mercy on the earth, the one we call home.

Are the characteristics just pointed out consistent with the girl in The Star being Inanna/Ishtar? Not entirely: that is to say, in some ways, but not in others. It may depend on how literal you want to be. As a mother type, and especially as a mother goddess, she was obviously nurturing in the broadest sense; but those features that make the Star image distinctive are not traceable to any known myths about Inanna.

Is it the case, then, that the image on The Star somehow derives from the image in Figure 4?

Yes. It is one of the source images.

Looking again at the cylinder seal, though, among the things that become apparent is that the crouching female figure has none of the specific elements in the card image just discussed. On the other hand, the figure from which the Death image was copied does appear to be doing something similar (to the activity of the figure in the card image) with a tree: he appears to be *cutting* it.

Does that make him, then, a woodcutter?

If it is assumed that it does, will it provide any clues to the identity of the female figure?

Assume, too, that the connection suggested – and not for the first time – between the content of these cylinder seals and the Sufis is a real one. Further, take note of the fact that some modern representatives of the Sufi tradition have maintained that what until recently had been assumed to be primitive, childish stories in the oral folklore traditions of people throughout the world contain a deep and valuable wisdom, if we only knew how to decode them.

Is there a story that some say is not only an example of such a form, but one of the most important? One that involves a woodcutter and a girl?

Although the story of Mushkil Gusha is almost certainly best known through the work of Idries Shah (*Caravan of Dreams*), it has survived through other presentations, sometimes with minor variations. It is usually called 'a story from Persia.' The tale is of a poor woodcutter who has a daughter. Every day he cuts wood in the forest, puts it into bundles, and carries it into the town, where he sells it. The problem is the daughter: she isn't satisfied with the food, and would like better. The only way the woodcutter can think of to go about this is to get more money by selling more wood, which means getting up earlier in order to cut more. He embarks on this program only to find himself and his daughter becoming increasingly out of synchrony, and he is, even, inadvertently locked out of their home. At his point of greatest exhaustion, he finds himself being addressed by a voice with an unseen source, which instructs him to climb invisible steps and gather the stones that he sees lying all around there. It gives him to understand that his fortune is being changed by the grace of 'Mushkil Gusha,' and that to ensure its continuation he should recite the story of Mushkil Gusha, telling how Mushkil

Gusha removed his difficulties.

The stones, once in the woodcutter and his daughter's house, turn into glowing jewels, which he then sells for a large sum of money. With that money he then buys them a fancy new dwelling directly facing the palace of the king, who also has a daughter. He forgets, however, the instructions about Mushkil Gusha.

While the woodcutter's daughter is swimming with the princess, the princess cannot find her necklace, and accuses the woodcutter's daughter of having stolen it, with the consequence that the woodcutter commences a further series of experiences, beginning with imprisonment.

The story would appear to be an allegory of spiritual development as the Sufis see it. It contains hints, in metaphorical form, of truths and, perhaps, instructions for aspirants not as memorably or concisely conveyable by means restricted to literal understanding of religious terminology. When seen for what it is, it indicates a level of sophistication not only far above that customarily attributed to our so-called primitive ancestors, but well beyond that of our own twenty-first century psychology (not to mention, indeed, the conventions of religion). If the figures in the cylinder seal are those of characters in an ancient version of the Mushkil Gusha tale, the implications on a number of levels are intriguing.

One of the discoveries of modern psychology is the extent to which humans can be, and almost invariably are, conditioned, and how what they think is their objective perception is mostly or altogether a result of conditioning from numerous sources. A spiritual teaching like Sufism would seem to aim, from one point of view, to free man from the limitations of that conditioning, so that the part of him that is capable of perceiving something beyond it – the relatively subtle – should be allowed to do so. As already mentioned, in Sufism, faculties in the individual that are activated are termed 'subtleties' (Arabic *lataif*). The notion of subtlety itself is one that it would probably be prudent to try and absorb and consider from different aspects.

What the woodcutter does with his wood is an allegorical description of what all of us do every day with the raw material of our experience. We trim off the bits that 'don't fit,' in order to be able to bind the larger pieces together into neat bundles for easy carrying: or if not exactly easy, at least it makes it possible. The material is then processed in such a way as to result, eventually, in a kind of nutrition: but the woodcutter's daughter, that aspect of the individual that craves higher perceptions ('finer food'), is not satisfied. Thus does the woodcutter, the part of the mind that acts in the world, set out to assuage his own spiritual hunger; but, the actor being of a different nature, his efforts by themselves fail, until the manifestation of whatever is meant by 'Mushkil Gusha.'

'Mushkil' means, in Arabic, 'difficulty' or 'problem,' and 'Gusha' is Persian for 'open.' The nearest Arabic equivalent of the sound of *gusha* means 'dispel.' It amounts to the same thing. In effect, when the characters in the story say, 'Our difficulties have been removed through Mushkil Gusha,' what they are literally saying is, 'Our difficulties have been removed through the remover of difficulties.' Before one assumes that this is an instance of primitives reveling in tautology, it might be worth considering it from the point of view of essential qualities, such as the Names spoken of before.

The stones the woodcutter is instructed to collect that are lying all around him on the ground in the other world that he enters at the behest of the voice are directly related – indeed, are, did he but realize, the same thing – as the bits of wood he trimmed off while doing his woodcutting. They represent things that we overlook, the things in our everyday life that aren't of any importance to us precisely because they don't seem to fit into our edited experience. Indeed, so much do they not fit that they are unconsciously dismissed and, in effect, not noticed at all: which is what is meant by cutting them off. They aren't necessary for living ordinary life with its ordinary 'food.' It is interesting that the Arabic words for 'stone' and 'jewel' have the same consonants in different arrangements, and another meaning of the word for 'jewel' (*jauhar*) is 'essence.'

The question of what 'not fitting' means is not as simple as it might appear, either. If something to which you have given little or no attention because you thought it was unimportant turns out to have more importance than you thought, it can be said to fit, in the sense that you are, at least, willing to entertain the idea that it might have a place somewhere, even if you don't yet know what that is. It may still, however, be said not to fit in the sense that its apparent potential value is incongruent with its modest presentation. If the time comes when you discover that it is far more valuable not only than you ever suspected, but than you are capable of appreciating, it may be said that it is, now, not the thing itself that doesn't fit, but you – because it is you who failed to appreciate it, and still can't quite understand it. The paradoxes and the ironies, and perhaps the meaning of the transformation itself of the stones into the jewels, are in jumping those gaps, and the first step in making the first jump may be in accepting the premise: the premise conveyed by the story.

Understanding the rest of the story requires a willingness to endure a discontinuity of context. The woodcutter and his daughter move into their big, palace-like house opposite the palace of the king. A basic teaching of Sufism concerns the stages of transformation of the self as it makes progress on the mystical path: the Arabic word *nafs* literally means 'breath,' but includes implications of 'soul' or 'self.' The lowest natural stage, and the one in which the mass of humanity spends all of its time, apparently, is the *nafs al ammara*, usually translated as 'commanding self.' It is portrayed in a variety of unflattering ways in Sufi analogical literature. One of the ways it is sometimes referred to is as a 'false king.'

Clearly, this is what is intended by juxtaposing the *nouveau riche* woodcutter with the real king. The next stage in the soul's upward progress is the *nafs al lawammah*, the 'accusing' or 'blaming self,' where the individual awakens to his short-comings. Again, this is obviously what is meant by the woodcutter's arrest and imprisonment; and the things that he does, and that happen to him in the remainder of the tale, correlate with further stages.

The fact that the woodcutter in the cylinder seal image is a deity should not be seen as precluding his also being a woodcutter if one only recalls some of the fun and games the gods and goddesses of, for instance, the classical pantheons got up to. If Hermes could be a cattle thief at the age of five minutes, why could not a Sumerian deity be a woodcutter?

It is striking, too, that at one point in the Mushkil Gusha story, the king's daughter, the princess – on the strength of whose accusation that the woodcutter's daughter has stolen her necklace while they were swimming the woodcutter was imprisoned – realizes her mistake when she is about to bathe in the stream again, and sees the reflection of the necklace hanging from the branch where she left it. She would, presumably, have been in a position much like the one of the female in Figure 4.

The image of the running stream is a metaphor also used by the great Andalusian Sufi philosopher Ibn 'al Arabi to represent consciousness, or a stage of development of it; the nature of the stage and the development is indicated, in its use in the story, by the fact that the princess and the woodcutter's daughter were in the stream, but are now not in it: in other words, the stream is the mind or heart of the mystic purged of the pollution of selfhood, so that it can now reflect a higher level of reality.

Having looked at the card, and thought about it, and looked at what was almost certainly one of the models for the pictorial content of the card, and thought about that as well, we still cannot say with certainty that a direct, intended link between the meaning of one and that of the other has been proven. It is precisely here, then, that the strong probability has to be allowed that the transition was not a fully informed one. There are images, and there are words, and whatever use has been made of what we have inherited in the form in which we have inherited it, the fact remains that, somewhere along the line, somebody almost certainly got their wires crossed.

Anyone who knows anything about Arabic knows that its words are formed from consonantal roots, and that those roots have multiple meanings. In their literature, moreover, Sufis make extensive use of more than one method of conveying meanings, including homonyms (words that sound alike but have different meanings), rhymes, re-ordering of those consonants, and a numerical cypher (the *abjad* system) based on the roots.

Any attempt to ferret out the contents of the basis for the Tarot cards thus cannot avoid referring to both the wordplay and word-mistake aspects.

Among the commonest Arabic words for 'star' is *falak*. Its connotations more broadly are of sphericity (the sphere of the sky) and of stellar influence (astrology). An associated meaning in connection with roundness is 'round breasts.'

A variation on the same root is *fuluka*, meaning 'ship' or 'barque.'

The female figure in the card is kneeling. 'Kneel' in Arabic is *barak*; and another meaning of *barak* is blessing, as in *barakat*, the power of the Sufis that vivifies and preserves. Another word with the same consonants in a different order is *bikr*, which means 'virgin' or 'maiden.' *Bakar* means 'rise early, happen early in the morning.' What the round breasted maiden, if she is one, on the card is doing as she kneels so early in the morning that the sun has not come up might be seen as administering a kind of blessing, and an interpretation in terms of Sufi metaphysics makes explicit and specific reference to the notion of 'the Blessed.' How these terms and ideas may link with the content of the cylinder seals is something that will appear later.

Figure 6. Detail showing battling gods from an Akkad period cylinder seal. British Museum.

Figure 7. Detail showing kneeling figure with star from Ur III period (before 2003 BCE) cylinder seal. British Museum.

Figure 6 shows part of another seal image in which some sort of a battle between deities is taking place – or, to be more precise, the victory of some gods over others: which gods, no one knows, nor the significance of the conflict. The position of the god on the left, wielding the mace, is obviously almost identical to that of the arboriculturally active one in Figure 2; and, especially in view of the content, a scene like the one in Figure 6 could, frankly, also have been a model for the Death card.

Figure 8. Detail of cylinder seal showing Inanna on her throne (not shown) with another goddess. Akkad period, 2330–2150 BCE. Private collection.

Figure 7 shows a worshipper with a star; and, apart from the raised arm, more hardly need be said about its relevance here. It is an example of how a Tarot image can be seen to have been, in all likelihood, the result of combining more than one source image from within the cylinder seal corpus.

In Figure 8 a female figure makes a ritual gesture, and pours a libation.

Before whom, and in worship of whom, does she do this?

Inanna. Ishtar.

The fact is, Mesopotamian cylinder seals have more people pouring things in them than the US Air Force has explanations for Roswell.

One more image is worth considering as a contributing source for this card.

A detail from another cylinder seal impression is shown (Figure 9), this time of the god called Enki by the Sumerians and Ea by the Semites: who, as Lord of the Deep, is depicted in his water-house. The person shown is some sort of attendant who appears to be grasping the erect pole supporting the roof.

Figure 9. Detail from Akkad period cylinder seal showing Ea (not shown). British Museum.

The image is also exactly identical to alternative versions of the Strength card in some older Tarot decks.

One Sumerian myth in particular involves a Tarot card already considered.

The interpretation of the Death card as representing transformation may be closer to the real, original truth than anyone suspects.

Consider the possibility that the artist responsible for it, while referring to the cylinder seal image already specified, and before the name 'Death' ever came to be associated with it, was trying to portray something like what is shown in the card, yet something that was also different from it in crucial ways.

Suppose that the instrument the figure is supposed to be wielding is not a sickle, but some other, not that dissimilar, tool: another agricultural implement, in fact.

Suppose those heads scattered on the ground are not the gruesome detritus of a massacre, but are where they are in the picture for another reason altogether.

Another important Mesopotamian myth concerns the god called Enlil by the Sumerians and Bel by their Semitic successors. As one of the trio of great Mesopotamian gods (the others being Anu, the Sumerian An, and Ea/Enki), he was the god of the air, and occupied a role that was, in a way, more important than that of An (even though An was considered the supreme god) because he, Enlil, while not having An's authority, was the god of force and power.

He was, in addition, the god of agriculture. In the Sumerian myth about the creation of the hoe, it is told how he sundered heaven and earth to make space for seeds to grow, and then, after inventing the hoe, used it to crack the hard surface of the ground. From the opening emerged mankind.

Assuming that this myth means something, what could it mean?

'It would be a ridiculous and unwarranted assumption,' wrote the pioneering psychologist Carl Jung, 'on our part if we imagined that we were more energetic or more intelligent than the men of the past.'[8]

Quite a number of people are going further and coming around to the view that the 'men of the past' knew things, very important things, that we do not, and that one of the ways they attempted to preserve and pass on their knowledge was in the form of allegories that our scholars call myths, and fairy tales, and so on. An example has already been found in the story of Mushkil Gusha.

If Blavatsky was on the right track, at the very least some of this Tarot material refers to matters usually called esoteric; and it may, further, partly deal with developments available – other things being equal – to man that involve his consciousness and its evolution.

Is it likely, then, that this myth, if it is an allegory, refers to some sort of actual physical creation of the first human beings? It does not look as if Jung would have thought so.

Man's mind or soul is sometimes spoken of as being covered or veiled, this veil or series of veils descending on him when he is born: his task then being, if he wants to attempt it, to remove those veils to restore direct contact with his extra dimensional origin. In this life, however, the covering is made thicker and tougher by a multitude of influences. Breaking through it may be the birth that is meant in the myth-story about Enlil, the Hoe, and Men.

Likewise, and what is more surprising, the Koran, in Sura 71, says: 'God made you come forth from the earth like plants'.

It was fundamental to Gurdjieff's teaching that there was a time when humanity had some form of direct contact with ranges of thinking and feeling above what is now assumed to be normal, and that the inner instrument by which that contact was effected was conscience. He spoke of conscience (often qualifying it with descriptors such as 'real' and 'objective,' just to point out that there might be more to what he meant than what we assume when we hear the word) as having been somehow engulfed or buried below the surface of consciousness, thus greatly facilitating its exclusion from the mental processes of day to day life. Any meaningful development of humanity's soul cannot, therefore, be hoped for without encompassing, at some early stage, the breaking-through, back to the surface, of conscience.

It is the stuff of classical tragedy as well as elementary psychology that conscience, when obscured by circumstances that don't challenge it – the life most of us, quite understandably, strive for most of the time, in fact – is disinterred by the experience of suffering. From Sophokles to *The Sopranos*, it is a fundamental theme.

In this context, what is represented in the Death card would appear to be nothing less than the emergence of man's real mind and self: with help from a higher level, such as a teacher and a teaching. 'Death,' in this sense, then, is really birth: clichés may be boring, but they are sometimes true.

Enlil being a god of energy and force but not authority may allude to the fact that such a breaking-through, when it occurs, cannot be counted on to do so in a way that is altogether convenient and without repercussions for what one feels to be the legitimate orderliness of one's life.

Wisdom traditions like Sufism seem to assert that the uncovering of what is sometimes called conscience is a first step; and even when, as today, they are sometimes considered independently of a religious context, the retention of the significance of conscience without necessarily depending on reference to whatever local morality prevails is explained in terms of its constituting a kind of objective alignment with the greater reality that is man's origin, and that itself is beyond all religions and systems of morality. It is probably easier, too, to say what 'objective alignment' does not mean than what it does: thinking one has succeeded in defining it in terms of relative ethics is, by definition, bound to fail. It can only be positively defined through reference to its own context, and knowledge of its context is, inevitably if ironically, a matter of experience.

Sufi literature abounds in references to the 'polishing' of the 'mirror' of man's inner being, of 'removing accretions' on it that obscure his perception. Ghazali, for instance, says: 'Most do not know the soul and its qualities, because a screen has been placed between it and their lower self...Rust accumulates on the soul unless it is removed by good actions and remorse. Dust on a mirror can be removed...Sufis have said that material possessions make the mind hard and despicable, and prevent it remembering God. They found that suffering softens and purifies the mind, and fits it for the reception of the grace that comes from remembrance of God.'

Hakim Sanai, before Rumi, likewise wrote how 'argument and dispute will not remove the rust of multiplicity and hypocrisy from the mirror of the heart...Vigorous refusal (of habituating influences) is the knife that will scrape existence from the mirror of the free (unconditioned perception).' The connection with what is today called conditioning is clearly stated by the early Islamic-era Sufi author Hujwiri: 'The soul loves custom, and becomes used to things; after a thing has become a habit, it quickly becomes a part of that soul's nature; and after that, it becomes a veil.'

Considering a fairly sophisticated symbolic use of story and image, then, as the one that may have been intended by our distant ancestors, it does rather make some of our self-appointed experts in more than one field look as if they are the ones obsessed with sex, fertility, planting in the spring, and Enlil knows what.

For the moment, though, let us continue to think about Ishtar, the Goddess of Love, and her lover Dumuzi, who, if he said, "Till death do us part,' was probably somewhat surprised to find that in his case it didn't.

Figure 10. Tarot. The Lovers.

Another example of the intensely enigmatic quality of the Tarot images that is, no doubt, at the heart of their appeal and endurance is that of the one on the card, 'The Lovers.'

It *says* 'Lovers,' but there are *three* people there: and that is not even counting the angel.

A romantic triangle? It looks like a man between two women, judging by their clothes.

The implication is obvious, and has been widely acknowledged by commentators on the Tarot: it means he has to make a choice, which, by definition, is a conscious activity. In other words, if the image and the name are to be accepted on their own merits, as a whole with no mistake and nothing added or missing, they are saying: 'Yes, this is about 'love,' but it is about love in relation to, involved with, the spirit or, at least, the mind; not straightforward and convenient exchange of body fluids, and probably including sacrifice' – because in choosing one, the individual in the middle will, obviously, be foregoing the other. It is that simple, and that complicated. The angel is there; and if the angel is Cupid (the arrow), it makes no difference, because it is only one arrow.

The Tarot cards are not the only cultural artifacts that at times resemble the proverbial camel drawn by a committee.

They have aspects that circumvent the front-line defense of the logical mind so that one does not notice they are now building cities, complete with apartment complexes and schools, in one's subconscious. (T. S. Eliot said something similar when, in *The Use of Poetry and the Use of Criticism*, he compared the overt meaning of a poem to a piece of meat thrown to a guard dog by a burglar in order to pacify and preoccupy it while the burglar, the real content of the poem, exerts its influence on the reader or hearer.) These are the arms that look like they must be broken, yet the brokenness of which seems to serve no function; the things that must be some kind of animal, yet are not identifiable as any known animal; and, for that matter, calling a picture of three people who look like they could be any three people having a conversation 'The Lovers.'

Before he became a character in a musical, the man history has taught us to call Jesus lived in the part of the world often called Palestine, and further comment in this regard is superfluous except to say that there is much evidence that: whether or not he was crucified, he did not die then, but travelled east, and lived into his seventies in what is now called Kashmir, having a family and fulfilling his mission to the lost tribes of Israel in that area and in what is now Afghanistan; and the material in the Gospels as defined by the Gnostic-fearing Irenaeus is neither complete, nor always accurate in what it does contain: the authorities who attended the Synod of Hippo and the Council of Carthage in the fourth century, and decided what was in the New Testament and what was not, were clearly extremely fallible people whose motives were, to put it mildly, not above suspicion.

It is also well known that the New Testament contains stories Jesus told, which are invariably called parables.

Feelings can be aroused by these parables, and other stories about Jesus that sound almost like parables-in-action, that are not dissimilar to those aroused by the Tarot cards. The explanations given *ad nauseam* by everyone from university theologians to the evangelist with a phone number under his face become less plausible the more closely they are examined. Whether they are just slightly off center or miss the mark completely, they are not very convincing; one cannot escape the feeling that the truth must be something else altogether, and probably involves information that we simply do not have.

One such account is in The Book of Matthew, Chapter 26, verses six to 13.

'Jesus was in the town of Bethany, eating at the home of Simon, who had leprosy. A woman came in with a bottle of expensive perfume and poured it on Jesus' head. But when his disciples saw this, they became angry and complained, 'Why such a waste? We could have sold this perfume for a lot of money and given it to the poor.' Jesus knew what they were thinking, and he said: 'Why are you bothering this woman? She has done a beautiful thing for me. You will always have the poor with you, but you won't always have me.''

The spoken language of both Jesus and his disciples was Aramaic, which was also one of the languages of Jewish sacred literature of their time. The religious and secular legal authorities interpreted the Hebrew biblical scriptures to the masses in

Aramaic. Hebrew, both historical and modern, has a great deal in common with the other great Semitic language, Arabic, a fact less surprising when one considers that they have a common ancestor that linguists, for lack of a better name, call Protosemitic.

Over the centuries of their existence up to the time of the writing of the books of the Bible – as, of course, in the time since – the Jewish people, whether through captivity or by other means, came into contact with a wide variety of foreign cultures and languages, and Hebrew was inevitably changed by those contacts. Arabic, on the other hand, was, until the time of the expansion of Islam, the language of a relatively isolated people. One consequence of these unarguable historical facts is that of existing languages, Arabic is likely to be the closest to Protosemitic. If knowledge or methods of encoding and accessing it, or both, were woven into Protosemitic, and they are to be sought in any currently used language, Arabic is the obvious choice.

If, moreover, the methods – the ones of which we may have an inkling, at any rate – used to embed knowledge in one place (such as Arabic) are tried out in another (such as ancient Hebrew writings), especially when the two are known to have a common ancestor, and the results appear meaningful, it is reasonable to conclude that the same methods were used to embed knowledge in that other place.

Anyone with even a rudimentary knowledge of these languages (and also of others, such as Greek), when examining ancient religious and other literature, cannot help but notice that there is an enormous amount of playing-on-words: with, on the most obvious level, extensive use of homonyms: in other words, punning.

That this practice continues in the present day in more than one circle is evident from a reading of the first work to be translated into English of the mysterious twentieth century French alchemist Fulcanelli, *Le Mystere des Cathedrales*: 'Truth, preserved in the speech of the common people, has ensured the continued use of the expression *gothic art*, in spite of the efforts of the Academy to substitute the term *ogival art*. There was an obscure reason for this, which should have made our linguists ponder, since they are always on the look-out for the derivation of words...For me, gothic art (*art gothique*) is simply a corruption of the word *argotique* (cant), which sounds exactly the same. This is in conformity with the *phonetic law*, which governs the traditional cabala in every language and does not pay any attention to spelling.'[9]

The woman poured perfume on Jesus' head. Arabic for 'perfume' is a word that may be transliterated *'itr*; probably everyone has heard of 'attar of roses.'

Another meaning of *'itr* is 'essence.' This is by no means farfetched, of course, since it is quite customary to refer to 'essences' in connection with perfume. There are, at the same time, other Arabic words that also mean 'essence,' just as in English.

Arabic for 'love' is *muhabbat*. (Another word is *'ishq*, but it has the connotation of 'excessive' or 'passionate.') A basic Sufi instruction manual is the *'Awarif al Ma'arif* (*Gifts of Gnosis*) by Shahab ad din Sahrawardi, following the formulations of an earlier Sufi, also called Sahrawardi, who was murdered for the threat he was considered to pose by the guardians of the social order of the time. In the section on *muhabbat*, he calls it the foundation of all sublime spiritual 'states' (*hal*), and defines it as the 'inclination' of the 'heart' (*qalb*) to the contemplation of beauty. Most interesting, however, is that he distinguishes between two kinds of love: love that is drawn to consideration of qualities or attributes; and love that contemplates the essence – in Arabic, *dhat*.

The more general kind of love, he says, is like a light that prettifies things, while the special, essential variety (and by nature the former is involved with multiplicity, and the latter seeks unity and the unique) is like a fire that purifies. The attribute-preoccupied love looks at the fine, and sees how it differs from the crude, and at lightness, and sees how it differs from heaviness; whereas love of the essential sees fineness within fineness, and lightness within lightness.

The *dhat* in this passage and the *'itr* in the story about Jesus (and, for that matter, the *jauhar* in the Mushkil Gusha story) all seem to mean more or less the same thing.

Sahrawardi goes on to tell a story about a man who saw a beautiful woman, and communicated his love to her. In reply she said that another woman, her sister, even more beautiful than herself, was standing near her. The man looked to see this other; whereupon the beautiful woman vented her fury, explaining to him that he was, in reality, neither a wise man, as she had supposed when she saw him from a distance, nor a lover, as she had thought when he came closer.

Looking again at The Lovers card, one feels one can almost hear them talking...

Jesus contrasts the essential love that the Sufis call 'special' with the 'love' – or what ought to be ordinary humanitarian compassion – of his other disciples for 'the poor.' If nothing else, it shows how careful you have to be with traditional religious materials. One might otherwise have been tempted to think that Jesus was saying it was not all that important to take care of the poor, because they'll always be around, which sounds and, indeed, would be callous; whereas, if our interpretation here is correct, in the context of the lesson the event is meant to impart, 'the poor' simply stands for something else.

It is, in other words, a kind of allegory. It also presents a compelling example of the shock tactics for which Sufis are famous: one can imagine the disconcertment of the conscientious and well meaning disciples at what they think is the suggestion that they should be indifferent to the poor; and if all that is not enough, it is an equally riveting illustration of the continuity of a teaching almost universally assumed to be the property of the adherents of whatever its most recent shell is.

The disposition of the three characters in the card invites us, whether intentionally or fortuitously, to elaborate further on this theme, and even points us in the direction.

Hujwiri connected the ideas of love and essence by saying that the love of the essential is the love of like towards like, exemplified in the love between humans that is the desire for the *dhat* of the beloved, to be obtained by sexual intercourse. It thus cannot be applied to ultimate reality, because God is unknowable in his essence; the most we can hope for is knowledge of his attributes. The other kind is love of that which is unlike oneself, and its goal is intimate attachment to the beloved's attributes, such as being attached to the lover's capacity to hear without oneself having the capacity to speak, or to her capacity to see without oneself having eyes. If this is confusing because these two ideas, about 'hearing' and 'seeing,' seem different, what they have in common is absolute concern for the object of love, and complete unconcern for the one who loves. The loved one's capacity to hear is valued, but not that what she hears should be the voice of the lover; likewise her capacity to see, but not the lover's capacity to see her. Where difference and attributes are involved, so are limitation and imperfection, which in themselves are foreign to divine reality.

Continuing the 'hearing and seeing' analogy, others, contrarily, say that *muhabbat* can arise through hearing (indirect experience, or experience of attributes), and can thus be said to apply to man's correct attitude to ultimate reality, which is inevitably circumscribed by his own limited nature, while *'ishq* cannot exist without direct experience (sight), and thus does not apply. A further refinement of the doctrine is that the 'excessive' nature of *'ishq* is exactly what makes it appropriate for love of God's essence, as it were, and is legitimate inasmuch as neither

excessive love nor God has an opposite. It is this latter formulation that would appear to be the one expressed in the Bible
story about Jesus and in Sahrawardi's illustrative tale.

A Sufi teacher named Sumnun al Muhibb asserted that both
the basis and the very principle of the way he taught were love –
'A thing is explainable,' he said, 'only by something subtler than
itself, and there is nothing subtler than love' – and that love is the
only state (*hal*) or station (*maqam*) that is indestructible, insofar as
the path or way itself is indestructible.

This notion of what or who is 'like' or 'unlike' the 'beloved' as
the object of the lover's love, in the context of these metaphysical
themes, is a potentially rich one through which to view The
Lovers card. The man is attracted to the woman – one of them, at
least! – and as far as that goes it is the attraction between entities
unalike; but from the point of view of essence seeking essence, it
is seeking the same. On the lover's other side is another woman,
whose very otherness suggests that, although she is like the first
woman, the one to whom the man is attracted, by virtue,
obviously, of her femaleness, it is yet not her femaleness that is of
significance in the context represented, which in turn implies
that the kind of 'love' meant in this case is also 'other,' in the
sense of being essential or 'spiritual': which is, however,
certainly not to say it is not experiential and, indeed, it would
appear to be to such real experiences that the Sufis allude,
whether or not the Tarot card does also. This, of course, in turn
raises the whole question of what 'essence' is, and its meaning,
and the means by which it might be indicated.

There is, then, the third figure: the 'third person singular'
(regardless of gender, and here is a possible link to the World
card). The *Dictionary of Islam* tells us that the Arabic word *hu* or
huwa is 'the personal pronoun of the third person, singular,
masculine, HE, i.e. God, or He is. It occurs in the Qur'an in this
sense, e.g. Surah iii. 1,...'God, there is no god but HE'...The word
is often used by Sufi mystics in this form: *ya hu, ya hu, ya man la*

ya'lamu ma hu illa hu, 'O He (who is), O He (who is), O He whom no one knows what He Himself is but Himself.''[10]

It is this 'He' whose name Sufis repeat in their *dhikr*, and this 'He'-Who-is-God that is even sometimes equated with *'ishq*. One of the better known *hadith* (recorded sayings of Mohammed) has it that, in answer to the prophet David, God said, 'I was a hidden treasure; I created the world because I wanted to be known.' The implication would seem to be that there is an inward and an outward aspect even where God is concerned. 'The inward is called *Huwiyyat*, He-ness, and the outward *Aniyyat*, I-ness. *Huwiyyat* represents the Thought of the Divine Mind turned in to the One and *Aniyyat* the Thought going out, as it were, to the realization or expression of itself in manifestation...*Huwiyyat* corresponds more to the *Hu* of the *dhikr*, where the aim is to put off the fetters of individuation and to be lost in the Hidden Oneness.'[11] The angel in the air over The Lovers may, if one is so inclined, be thought of as representing this hidden oneness.

Figure 11. Detail from Sippar, circa 870 BCE, stele showing Nabuplaiddin being presented to Shamash (not shown).

Not all the Mesopotamian art interesting from the point of view of its potential relevance to the Tarot cards is on cylinder seals. Figure 11 shows part of an image atop a stele, or standing stone slab, on which the king of the time, Nabuplaiddin, recorded for posterity how he restored the image of the sun god and his temple. Presentation scenes are common in Mesopotamian art. There were, in the pantheon of the nation, those very great deities in whose hands rested the fate of the nation and, ultimately, the fates of the individuals within it. Between those high gods and mortals, however – beginning with the king himself, and devolving downward – were somewhat lesser

40

divinities who acted as intermediating agencies. They are usually female, and are depicted with a firm grip on the wrist of the supplicant as they introduce him to the major-league god or goddess; Ishtar, in particular, is frequently shown interceding for the monarch in this manner.

In Figure 11 we see the king, the one in the middle, with his two escorts, who are divinities in their own right. The round object on the table the leg of which the individual in the front is grasping is a sun-disk, an emblem of the god Shamash, the great god to whom the king is being presented. About the odd bearded fellows in the upper right, even what significance it may be possible to gather in the context of the stele image cannot be considered here, because what is shown here is only that part of the scene that is likely to have been the origin of the image on the card The Lovers. It requires no great effort of imagination to see how the figures aloft who seem to be executing some procedure with some kind of ropes extending down to the sun-disk have become the arrow-shooting angel, and the sun-disk the angel's nimbus. The three figures who seem unable to keep their hands off each other are, of course, the three 'Lovers.'

There are, again, many cylinder seals that bear presentation scenes, and they are mostly quite similar. It seems likely that if any one artifact was the original for the card image, it was this one, for the reasons already given, and for more yet to be divulged.

Uncovering the next step in this process involves narrowing the focus on the image just considered: discovering by exclusion.

Delete the character on the extreme left; delete the strange

Figure 12. Detail of stele showing presentation to Shamash with sun-disk.

Figure 13. Tarot. The Sun.

pair in the air. Keep the two standing individuals and the sundisk.

What do we have?

Same people; different card (Figure 13). Same sun. It is even apparent that the horizontal lines of the support for the sundisk have transmogrified into the brick wall behind the two friends.

It is, again, worth keeping in mind that just because we accept that whoever produced the drawings that formed the images on the Marseille Tarot a few hundred years ago did so, apparently, by referring to some version of these ancient Mesopotamian images, we still do not know in what context he himself was working or thought he was working, or to what purpose. Indeed, short of some proof from someone who can also prove he was in the room at the time, it is difficult to see how it could be known with absolute certainty.

The Sun card has popularly been interpreted as an indication of harmony, happiness and all sorts of good things. The wall behind them suggests constructive activity, just as the sun stimulates growth in nature: and there is no reason to discount these ideas.

It is interesting, too, to consider the image from the point of view of the duality of the human figures (who are often taken to be children: again, not inconsistent with the themes of bliss and growth, and extending them to innocence) as contrasted with the unity and singleness of the sun: a perennial symbol for transcendent reality, which is, by its nature, unitive.

Jalaluddin Rumi wrote, in Persian, books that are (as already observed) now so well known in one form or another to students of mysticism in general, let alone of Sufism or Islamic civilization, that they hardly require introduction. At a certain stage in his life an enigmatic individual, a dervish with the name Shamsuddin Tabrizi – which literally translates as 'Sun of the Faith of Tabriz' (Tabriz being a city in Persia) – appeared out of nowhere, became his confidant and, perhaps, teacher, and then, after a few years, disappeared again. (Some say he was murdered by some of Rumi's jealous followers: which raises the question of what so exalted a teacher as Rumi was doing with such bloodthirsty people as disciples.)

Rumi composed a sequence of poems in praise of Shams. One such reads:

> Abolish duality have I done,
> Grasped that both the worlds are one.
> One I see and one I know:
> One I say, to find one I go.
> From the cup of love I took a sip –
> I'm drunk; I've given two worlds the slip.
> There's nothing left for me to do
> But let the partying continue.
> Hey, Shams, you from Tabriz,
> In this world I'm so pickled
> That, except to say, 'More, please!'
> I find nothing to be chronicled!

The 'drunkenness' Rumi means is the ecstatic experience – the *hal* – that descends unpredictably on dervishes as a result of their disciplines.

Shams, then, is Arabic for 'sun,' and 'Shamash' was the name of the god portrayed on the stele from which the image on the card appears to have been copied. While the possibility that the two figures are struggling cannot be discounted, the context suggests otherwise. They could represent any two people in a state of concord, harmony, friendship, whether or not any allusion to Rumi and Shams is involved. (It could also, for that matter, be Gilgamesh and Enkidu, whose significance will be considered soon.) If all nuances of the image are to be felt, though, one should not stop there: why should all this niceness be linked so conspicuously with the celestial orb at the center of our planetary system? If the relationship of life with the sun is as much of a cliché as all that, why bother to mention it?

The development of modern physics is in some ways the story of the idea of energy becoming more intelligible through its continual refinement. The Greek *energeia*, as used by Aristotle, was applied by Thomas Young in the early nineteenth century to what would today probably be thought of as something like the expression of energy in visible change. For centuries the term *dunamis*, sometimes translated 'force,' corresponded more closely to the property of a thing of being able to cause such change; the difference with current (post-Einstein) concepts of energy becomes evident when the thread of meaning of this term is traced to its origin: in this case, to a political reality, the concept of sovereignty. The idea of sovereignty itself, obviously, origi-nates in the reality of a sovereign. The reality of an ancient sovereign, a 'potentate,' may have had its own origin in – again – the force of the arms of his soldiers, which leaves the question of the nature of the force he held personally over them: which, again, disappears into the intangible, much as a relativistic atom-particle disappears into the intangibility of a wave when looked at through the lens of quantum physics; or, it may disappear into another kind of energy, such as was attributed to the godlike monarchs of ancient cultures, which are usually assumed to be embellishments of and for our benighted forefathers. If there are references to what would today be meant by 'energy' (in other words, what matter is when it isn't being matter) in cultures that did not include the term or the concepts needed for it, they will, obviously, be in other terms: for example, the Chinese *qi* (although study of some of the contexts in which it is used suggests that it is, ultimately, untranslatable). In many quarters, the recognition has long since occurred – witness, for example, eminent physicist Neils Bohr's personal emblem incorporating the Taoist yin-yang symbol – that these more traditional terms include reference to subtle forms of energy that are not fictitious simply because we do not yet have the means to study them as we are accustomed to studying things.

Perhaps there is a juxtaposition so close here as to be all but invisible.

The sun causes life; the sun causes harmony amid that life.

Or whatever is represented by the sun?

Just as important – are those not two different things?

Were it true, say, that there are what we would today call energies that produce the situation shown on the Sun card, would we know it? Assuming that we could accept the hypothesis, would we have any idea of their nature or source?

Yet another nuance of the picture of two entities in some sort of agreement is what might be called agreement in time – simultaneity or synchronicity – or, even, agreement in form across, or outside of, time: which, for instance, is the basis of metaphor and, further, leads us into considering the very nature of our thoughts and of mind itself; and, further still, into what Sufis call the *'alam al mithal*, the 'World of Similitudes.'

A Sufi teacher who died some years ago is reported, in the context of a conversation about 'coincidences,' to have said: 'This is the manifestation of a force without which there might be no life on this planet.'

While 'Shamash' is the name of the god, it is not unlikely that the name for this card comes from *sharq*, which, in addition to meaning 'sun,' also means 'sun*rise*.' One reason for thinking so is that a close homonym, *shirk*, means 'fellowship, company, association.' Another reason is that another important cylinder seal to be examined soon does actually portray the sun coming up.

A further way of considering this image, apparently so simple and yet so rich (especially relative to everything else so far discussed), is to pay more attention to the brick wall behind them and reflect on the fact that there are two of them, similar in appearance; and then to take all of this into account in the context of Mesopotamian myth.

A significant but relatively ignored example of such a myth – although not by Muslims, since it is mentioned in the Koran – is the one about Harut and Marut. There will be cause to go into that story in more detail later but, for the moment, it is worth noting that they were an angelic duo who expressed contempt for the weakness of mankind; God then arranged for them to have the experience of being human so they could see what it is like. They quickly became involved with a *femme fatale* type who would appear to have much in common with the goddess Ishtar. She led them into performing various regrettable acts, and when God offered them a choice of punishment – temporary now, or eternal later – they chose the former.

The place of their punishment was Babel: where, of course, there was a certain tower.

Shamash (the Sumerians called him Utu) was the bringer of light in more than the literal sense. He also did away with symbolic darkness, with disease and injustice, and was the champion of the oppressed and the disadvantaged. The vast comprehensiveness of his daily span across the sky and, especially, his unseen course beneath the world of men every night emphasized his thorough cognizance of all, including concealed, inequities, and even the king answered to him in such

matters.

Another representation of Shamash is shown in Figure 14. Rays emanate from his shoulders, and he holds up his symbol, a saw.

Figure 14. Detail from Akkad period (2250 BCE) cylinder seal showing Shamash rising between two mountains. British Museum.

The Tarot Magician stands before his table – recall the table in front of Shamash, the one supporting the sun-disk – and he holds up *his* symbol, or instrument: a wand.

There are people who do not 'believe in magic,' and there are people who do; and there are those who eschew belief as much as they can, and try to look at the evidence. In this as in so many areas, the ability to produce the appearance of something does not disprove the possibility of the existence of the reality.

Figure 15. Tarot. The Magician.

One of the popular interpretations of the Magician card is as indicating the presence of deception.

The philosophical principle that dates from the European Middle Ages and is referred to as Occam's Razor states that if there is a simple explanation for something, you should not seek a more complicated one.

The obvious defect of this principle is that one's very notion of what constitutes simplicity is itself almost certainly heavily culturally conditioned: which is to say it rests on a foundation of relative ignorance that is felt, on the contrary, to be a foundation of relative knowledge.

Another way of putting it might be to say that Occam's Razor is fine for shaving, but try to use it to do something requiring a finer instrument, such as brain surgery, and you will discover its limitations.

Your patient will not, however: because he will be dead.

Yet another way of looking at it is to say that one is less likely to stray into the area of impromptu plastic surgery on oneself while shaving if one does so with the benefit of a mirror. Context is required. Demonstrate the use of a television set to a Stone Age tribesman and, for him, the simplest explanation will be that it is haunted by ghosts. The correct, and much more complicated, explanation depends on having information that the tribesman does not have. Unfortunately, if he insists on only applying Occam's Razor, no doubt thinking himself a great scientist, he will never get that far.

Among those who do, at the very least, try to have an open mind about the possibility of paranormal phenomena – of which magic must be considered a variety – are those who view it as an end in itself, and others who see magical effects as by-products of a more comprehensive development. In the former category are those who follow various occult traditions, many of whom refer to the Tarot quite extensively and try to incorporate it into their theories and rituals, especially in combination with the Kabbalah. Where these authors have had anything interesting to say about the Tarot, it may be because they were covertly fed data that were intentionally partial or misleading, so that the schemes they present have to be viewed as, at best, forced, garbled and partly invented.

There is, then, more than one word in Arabic for 'sun,' and one of them also means 'sunrise.' Another word, also meaning 'sun,' is *sahar*; *suhara*, from the same root, means 'magician.' *Shahar*, similar in sound but from a different root, has as its first meaning 'to publish, spread abroad, make known'; and, as its second one, 'brandish the sword or knife (against),' just as Shamash appears to be brandishing his saw. *Shahr*, from the same root as *shahar*, means 'moon.' Moreover, another Arabic word, *nashar*, means both 'publish' and 'saw'. The connotations of 'magic' here are of deception, delusion, illusion.

Literature on the Sufis is so replete with descriptions of the deeds of Sufi masters that might well appear to amount to magic as to make mention of it almost redundant. They usually say, however, that actions they perform that seem to defy natural law are always to a purpose within a larger frame of reference.

In the context of the snapshots, as it were, of the ancient Mesopotamian culture in the cylinder seal impressions and other artifacts, it should not come as a great surprise that the idea of a figure we might, for lack of a better word, call a magician existed: who, in his capacity as an intermediary between ordinary mortals and the supernatural world, was also something like a priest. Indeed, the words 'magic' and 'magician' derive from the 'magi' (individual 'magus') who were the priests of the Zoroastrian religion of the Persians, who, as already noted, eventually conquered the area in which these seals originated.

Figure 16. Assyrian ninth or eighth century BCE cylinder seal showing a priest or worshipper with symbols of various deities, and a temple tower. Vorderasiatisches Museum, Berlin.

Figures 16, 17 and 18 show such individuals. The first two also, obviously, contain motifs that strongly suggest another Tarot card, The Tower. Figure 18 shows a priest before a fire altar; it seems likely that the flames flickering at an angle out of

Figure 17. Assyrian ninth or eighth century BCE cylinder seal showing a priest in front of a temple tower and a fox catching a fish. Vorderasiatisches Museum, Berlin.

the altar have become conflated with another image that is undoubtedly the main source of what is seen in the card (Figure 19).

Looking again at the image of what has universally been interpreted as a tower struck by lightning, what may strike us is the fact that the object – or phenomenon, if you insist on seeing

Figure 18. Akkad period cylinder seal showing a hierophant at a fire altar, the snake god, and a gate. British Museum.

Figure 19. Akkad period cylinder seal showing a winged gate on the back of a bull. British Museum.

Figure 20. Tarot. The Tower.

it as lightning – that seems to be causing the destruction resembles nothing so much as a gigantic feather.

The winged gate or door (Figure 20) is one of the motifs that occur over and over again in Mesopotamian seals for which no one seems yet to have come up with a satisfying explanation. (In Islam there is something called the *bab al abwab*, the 'door of heaven'; and the notion that the mundane world temporarily becomes, in unpredictable times and places, a medium by which something beyond itself can be perceived is inherent in Sufi metaphysics.) Again, once we know where to look, the correspondence is overwhelmingly clear: the Tarot artist, knowingly or otherwise, has mixed up the wing on the rectangular door, the fire atop the tall altar, and the literary references to a tower and to cities and peoples destroyed by divine decree.

The image on the card shows a structure, a tower, being struck by lightning and crumbling, with human figures falling head first from it. The most powerful association this has for us is with the Tower of Babel, the story of which is told in Genesis, of course, and which, as noted, was already current in ancient Babylon. In the story, humanity tried to build 'a city with a tower,' and God inflicted the 'confusion of tongues,' so that they could no longer understand each other and would thus, presumably, quit making towers – or, at least, that particular one. (What sort of activities they were expected to take up to fill their newly available time is not so clear.)

Two aspects of the possible significance of the story, and thus of the image, may be found in, first, considering the notion that the tower represents an aspect of human civilization that has become undesirable from the point of view of man's overall evolution or, even, survival.

Among the things that certainly need to be noted are the reasons given by the builders themselves, according to Genesis: 'We'll become famous, and we won't be scattered all over the world.' Just as interesting is the reason given by God for stymieing them: 'soon they will be able to do anything they want.' The method he used was to somehow cause them to cease to understand one another's speech, and the consequence was that they did, indeed, scatter across the earth. The Arabic *balbal* means 'confusion,' and also 'anxiety, sorrow,' and 'difference of opinions.'

It does not actually say that God – or anyone else – destroyed the tower. Moreover, the builders were building not 'a tower,' specifically, but 'a city with a tower.' 'Tower' in Arabic is *buruj*, which also means 'stations of the zodiac; angle; support,' and 'supreme power.'

The inference from these data would seem clear: they were prevented from doing what they wanted to do because, quite simply, a higher power intended something else. The 'supreme power' that would have accompanied (in their own minds, at least) the attainment of their goals – which, let us not deny it, sound like the very definition of civilization within a frame of reference that excludes any consideration of the 'other dimensions' discussed under the rubric of The Star – was incompatible with, was somehow out of alignment with, the bigger picture that, whether they liked it or not, not only includes those dimensions, but by comparison with which what we think of as the whole world is of little consequence. Their ideas about success were at odds with the greater reality: so the greater reality intervened to prevent their realization. One result of this was their dispersal: amounting, one may surmise, to their return to a status of something like raw material, possibly for subsequent use for later, correctly aligned, objectives.

If it is true that the Sufis, or some Sufis, are the preservers of an ancient knowledge not all of which comes under the heading of their own name for their path (*tasawwuf*), and that the Tarot, or that from which the Tarot derives, contains some of that knowledge, it may be that they are, in this case, telling us that what we think of as the priorities and goals of our uninformed world, the goals we take as self evidently desirable and important, are entirely expendable in the cosmic plan.

This, it hardly needs to be said, is something about which little useful comment is possible, since there is no way to confirm it; but it does constitute an interesting piece in the jigsaw puzzle of the meaning of the Tarot cards.

Islamic tradition contains references to ancient societies and peoples who were, frankly, destroyed, apparently for their failure to maintain an acceptable degree of alignment, even when informed explicitly that they had to, and were given opportunity to do so.

The Koran tells of the 'Ad and Thamud peoples, of south and north western Arabia, respectively, who were 'warned' by prophets – Hud ('Thamud' and 'Hud' both rhyme with 'mood') in the case of 'Ad, and Salih for the Thamud – that they had to change the way they did things. 'Ad, whose people were apparently known for their tallness, had become polytheistic, and the Thamud had allowed oppression of the poor by the wealthy classes to flourish. 'Ad was destroyed by 'a hot wind,' and Thamud by 'a mighty noise' accompanying an earthquake. A city named Iram, evidently of the 'Ad people, is called 'of the lofty pillars' or 'columns.' Muslim tradition also accords with that of the Jews on the nature of the misdeeds in Sodom (words similar to 'Sadum' mean 'sad, repenting, anger, abhorrence, be eager for') and Gomorrah (*ghamurah*, 'ill will'): which, of course, were also destroyed.

If the event the artist of the Tower card was attempting to portray was what happened to 'Ad, the name of the card The Lovers could be a misreading of it, because *'auda*, from *wadid*, means 'lovers.' Further, another homonym, *ad*, means 'break into pieces' (as well as 'number'); *'ad* means 'calamity'; *wada'* means 'to humble', and *wada* means 'to level, plane.'

As to the significance of the event, or the story based on the event, or the card based on the story – if the assumption is justified that a verdict of unviable social growth or behavior would be precluded by enough people (recall Abraham bargaining with God to spare Sodom) who were, as it were, in tune with the impulses of a more rarefied nature from the unseen world that is the source of the seen one – is there anything in the material under consideration to warrant it?

As already noted, a recurring theme in Sufi literature is the idea that development of man's consciousness will involve becoming aware of subtleties, and that a primary obstacle to doing this is his own unrefined ego, or commanding self. Subtlety would appear to be often represented – metaphorically, according to your precise definition of it – by qualities like smallness, lightness, delicacy, vulnerability, humility and so on, and the commanding self to invite representation by, conversely, bigness, coarseness, dominance, and similar things.

A possible example is the story of David and Goliath, where David (Arabic *didd*, 'adversary, opponent'), the young shepherd – a smaller person and a relatively pacific occupation involving caring for vulnerable animals – slings a stone – a small object – into the forehead (the location of the subtle faculty, or *latif*, corresponding to 'intuition') of the domineering giant Goliath (Arabic *ghilaz*, 'grossness, coarseness, harshness, ruthlessness, rudeness').

In addition to being the name of the prophet who warned the proud 'Ad, *haud* means 'affection, kindness' and, 'speaking quietly and gently.' *Wahid*, moreover, means 'one'; the 'Ad's overriding sin, apparently, was their polytheism: a small number (the smallest, in fact), a big number. *Ayeed* means 'do again or repeatedly'; the Thamud, it is stated, took the place of the 'Ad in some larger plan or purpose.

In the story of the equally proud Thamud, as told in the Koran, the test they failed was when a 'she-camel' (*naqat*) – which the Koran states explicitly was 'a sign' and 'a symbol' for them – was 'hamstrung' (instead of letting it drink from the water supposedly provided for all). *Naqt*, a different word but sounding almost exactly the same, means 'dot, spot, point, drop.' Sufis say that there is an 'arc of descent' of the human soul into this world, and the 'arc of ascent' that not everyone makes, but which is of the nature of the task of becoming a Sufi. That arc begins as a point that becomes a line. The downward journey, moreover, is sometimes described as 'the journey of the ocean towards the drop'; the journey of the seeker up is 'the journey of the drop towards the ocean.' *Niqat*, too, means 'dainty, taste.'

Abraham bargained with God – down, from a big number to a relatively small one (ten) – for the minimum number of 'good' or 'righteous' inhabitants of Sodom for whom he would spare it. Arabic for 'ten' is *'ashar*; *sirr* is 'secret, hidden thought, mystery; innermost and best part'; and another meaning of *'ashar* is 'fragment, piece.' The bargaining down might thus be seen, too, as a process of refinement to vanishing point, and the subsequent vanishing of Sodom, even, from this point of view, as a successful outcome.

Lut (rhymes with 'loot'), or Lot, was the warner only of his own family and their loved ones, and was spurred on by angels, who were disguised as human strangers; *'alat* means 'thread, gossamer' – Sufis speak of a hidden 'thread' through the labyrinth of events and things; and *'alalat* means 'distraction, diversion' (like the destruction of Sodom for Lot's wife when she stopped to look back) and, also, 'remainder, a drop,' with the same connotation. Lot flees to 'Zoar': the Arabic *su'r* meaning (again) 'anything left, remainder.'

The transgression of the Thamud people was revealed when they defied a divine decree to share water among all classes of society; *thamad* means 'find and preserve water' (rather than using it and leaving *'a remainder'*) and, also, 'take everything from, exhaust.'

Where the 'Ad reveled in their majestic, skyward reaching structures (*'amud,* 'pillars' or 'columns'), the Thamud (*tam* means 'finish, complete': *tam-amud,* 'end of the people of the pillars'? 'completion of the stage of erecting columns'?) carved dwellings out of stone, and rejoiced in their agricultural skills. Were their respective unbalanced tendencies opposites, and the means of their destruction – read 'correction'? – wind and earthquake, corresponding?

If an attempt to generalize and discern a pattern here may be allowed, it might be said that the people of 'Ad were wholly preoccupied with external achievement and were, thus, useless; the Thamud who replaced them were not so entirely given over to material accomplishment – the 'water' that they failed to share equitably might be taken to represent the stream of esoteric teaching – yet they did not use the opportunity they had to 'feed' the 'she-camel of God.' Where the 'Ad were devoted to 'many gods,' and the Thamud did not make use of what teaching they had, the Sodomites, the 'people of Lut,' transgressed against *strangers* (who, again, were really angels), and sought to do with them what they always did: put like with like in a way that, to say no more, was sterile. They may be said to have been unable or unwilling (it amounts to the same thing) to accept new teaching; and, from a certain point of view, all real teaching is new. Next came the Midianites, warned by Shu'aib, whose error was in failing to 'give full measure' in their commercial dealings – they knew of the essential 'balance' (an inherently delicate thing) to be observed and prized, but didn't prize or even observe it; they may have 'fed' their 'she-camel,' but not enough, and they also, according to the Koran, 'lay in waiting for wayfarers by night' to mislead them. They accepted, but distorted.

There is no question of the validity of the notion of the importance of what Sufis call *ma'arif* (gnosis) within, even, the broader religious context. Ghazali's *Ihya* is accepted as a foundation of Islamic religious thinking, and in it he made clear that (quoting Ibn Abbas) 'God will place the learned believers on a level seven hundred degrees over the ordinary ones.'

It is possible that the meaning of another great contemporary mystery is to be found by considering it within the context of the idea that informs these tales of errant proliferation corrected or, if you like, pruned by a kind of cosmic gardener or gardeners.

In recent decades the phenomenon known as crop circles has spread throughout much of the world, although the pictographs, which are often complex and not circles at all, continue to appear in their greatest numbers in western Europe, especially Britain, and North America. Some are certainly – and easily detected – hoaxes, but others have characteristics impossible to explain, including changes on the cellular level in the flattened crops, anomalous electromagnetic effects, the bodies of small wild animals (porcupines) within the area that have been squashed and spread such as would only be possible if done by a tremendous physical force, and other things. People have reported unexplained lights in the sky where the pictographs are later found, and others report having actually witnessed them in the process of instantaneous formation accompanied by such lights and heat.

If we assume that there is an intelligence of some kind producing these figures, and further assume that their purpose is to communicate something, the absence of any agreed-upon language for that communication can logically lead us to infer only one thing: namely, that the language being used is the language of symbolism, and it is the phenomenon itself that is the symbol.

Approaching the crop circle phenomenon as a symbolic communication, then, how do we read it?

The crops themselves are, in the most basic sense, growing things. They are things that grow, as it were (within the parameters of the given field, of course), without order, purpose or organization. For a complex pattern to be imposed on them as if from out of nowhere indicates a transcendent imperative for that order and purpose or, if you like, design. In the process of the imposition of this design, there is something like destruction involved – the destruction of the crops that are flattened.

If we take the crops as representing us, humanity, the message could hardly be clearer. If we don't do something about our own unchecked and mindless growth, it will be done for and to us; and, as with the crops, destruction will be involved.

Yet another, even opposite, context in which to consider the Tower image, one especially contiguous with the Middle Eastern mystical set of associations, is that of the reports of 'power houses' that are said to be real, material edifices of one kind or another with the purpose, overt or otherwise, of acting as some kind of transmitting stations for what would appear to be a subtle energy or energies that, in turn, may be under some sort of conscious control by persons unknown to equally obscure ends. In other words, it isn't a lightning bolt hitting the tower, it is something going the other way.

Researchers into energies emitted by Neolithic monuments and nexuses of ley lines may be contributing to the creation of a context in which to think about references to spiritual power houses, whose power is benevolent and, even, necessary for life. Historic structures such as the pyramids of past civilizations, it has been suggested, are examples of such benign power houses, ones that may have survived the limits of their usefulness in that regard.

Meanwhile, however, in his book *Adventures in Arabia: Among the Bedouins, Druses, Whirling Dervishes and Yezidee Devil Worshipers*, first published in 1925, the American traveler William Seabrook describes how a certain Turkish officer told him of his time among the Yezidis in Iraq, and how he had seen one of their fabled Seven Towers, or 'Power Houses,' lofty, white, and conical erections the pinnacles of which emitted blinding rays of light. According to Seabrook, the legend as he had heard it was that a string of seven towers atop mountains stretched from Manchuria to Kurdistan (now part of northern Iraq), taking in Tibet and Iran along the way. A supposed hierophant of Satan had his digs in each one, and sent out wicked occult vibrations the purpose of which was, needless to say, the perversion of the world. The Turk assured Seabrook that, whatever the true purpose of the towers was, they certainly existed, and he had seen them.

The American later went and viewed one of the towers for himself. Shaped, he says, like the sharpened point of a pencil, it was white and fluted (vertically grooved). Blinding flashes of light, heliograph-like, emanated toward him. Entering the tower, he found a compartment where the *kolchaks*, or Yezidi *fakirs*, took up residence for days on end and, presumably, went about their occult ways.

(The correspondences between the Satan of Islamic tradition and the Satan of the Yezidis are extensive, except that for the Yezidis he, or it, is not evil. His other name is Malik Taus, or Peacock Angel, and as such he is one of several spiritual potencies created by the supreme deity. Refreshingly to the modern sensibility, the Yezidis, in fact, hold that the real source of evil is man himself.)

Then again, there are stories about Sufis in which the Old Fellow is represented as a figure at least as deserving of pity as of anything else.

Then again, too, it appears that Seabrook was a bondage fetishist, and perhaps one ought not to discount the possibility that the Turkish officer noticed that, and simply told him a tale he thought he would enjoy.

Foxes and fishes: the graphic footnote in Figure 17.

The Moon.

Only in the picture on the card, they seem to be dogs or, maybe, wolves. Also a crab: well, it is something that lives in the water.

Even confining ourselves to the cylinder seals and other Mesopotamian artifacts as the origin of the images themselves, if not, necessarily, of their arrangement and **Figure 21. Tarot.** meaning, it is, as has been shown, evident **The Moon.** that elements from more than one source have been combined; so it is not too surprising to find it here as well. Examine a larger number of seals, and you will see that some have quite a lot of wildlife in them. Various scholars have felt confident in asserting that this or that animal or bird is the symbol of such-and-such a deity. It is very difficult to imagine that whoever did the cribbing for the Tarot cards, with the (what may fairly be called) added ingredient of chaos that has been apparent in the arrangement of the visual elements, realized that, however; and much less that they took it into consideration.

The dogs or wolves seem to be howling at the moon: which, if it did not say, 'The Moon,' you might be forgiven for assuming was the sun, since it seems to be blazing away, and the sky does not look dark. The beasts are between two towers and, in the foreground – or what our eye assumes must be a foreground – is some water, with crustacean ensconced in the middle. At the very bottom are some odd shapes that, with no additional information, one is inclined to assume must be rocks.

The scene as a whole suggests decay and ruin, and modern interpreters of the card have emphasized this aspect of it. One supposes that where there are wolves or dogs making that much noise, there are unlikely to be people (unless, of course, you have ever been to Penge); and yet the presence of the towers indicates that people were there once. In psychological terms, there would seem to be some justification for connecting this with the human unconscious, with dreams and ancient symbols that do not acknowledge the civilized rule of daytime consciousness, with the unilluminated side of mentation. The water, too, evokes invisible depths and the inchoate origin of all things.

Nanna, as he was known to the Sumerians (Sin to the Babylonians), was the Mesopotamian god of the moon. His symbol was the crescent, and he was believed to ride in it, as in a boat, across the sky. According to some myths, he was the son of Enlil and the father of Shamash, and rode a winged bull.

One of the odd doctrines taught by the mystic George Gurdjieff, who is known to have, at minimum, been heavily influenced by Sufis – apparently authoritative published opinions on this score fill the spectrum, from his having been a deliberate and knowing emissary to his having been a gifted maverick trying to implement incompletely learned and imperfectly understood teachings – concerned the role of the moon in relation to the Earth and, especially, humanity and its evolution.

The sun, the planets of the solar system collectively, and the earth individually combine, said Gurdjieff, to produce an energy that the earth transmits to the moon, and upon which the moon subsists and grows. The energy in question is gathered and stored in an apparatus on the surface of the earth, and that apparatus is none other than what Gurdjieff called 'organic life.' From this point of view, then, the great – or not so great, if you thought it was something else – purpose of organic life on earth, including the human race, is to provide sustenance for the moon. The notion of all that lives (organically, anyway, whatever 'non-organic life' might mean) on our planet being dedicated, unbeknownst to itself, to such a grim end, not to mention the idea of the moon being a celestial hungry stomach, is disconcerting, to say the least. It also tends to enhance any sense of urgency that may have been lacking with regard to the desirability of mental or, if one prefers, spiritual growth, which in this context constitutes liberation from the cosmically decreed lunar imperative. To be enmeshed in the habituating and mechanical forces already discussed is to have a place in the moon's diet, and becoming free from it is what accompanies the growth of consciousness.

Before one dismisses this as obvious nonsense, it may be worth bearing in mind that much of what Gurdjieff taught about psychology has been considered commonplace since the Behaviorists, and that among the ideas included in his major written work, *Beelzebub's Tales to His Grandson*, and that were thought bizarre at the time, is that the moon was once part of the earth, and was torn away from it as a consequence of an impact with a comet.

Since the Apollo missions, this view of the origin of the moon has been widely accepted.

Gurdjieff died in 1949. How did he know?

Preclassical and classical authors from Anaxagoras to Ovid, including Aristotle and Herodotus, refer to humans of an antiquity so remote that the earth they inhabited was one without a moon.

Whether or not university sociologists, moreover, think they have proven statistically that people do not go even crazier than usual when the moon is full, our long-suffering police and the people who tend to the needs of the mentally unbalanced are in no doubt.

The good news about The Moon, if not about the moon, is that we are free to think of it in other terms – and doing so may be an example of developing those very faculties of which Gurdjieff spoke; we can view it, for instance, as the source of the light that enables us to see when there is no light of the kind we are accustomed to thinking of as the only kind: and which, as such, is that much more important.

The atmosphere in the card does, however, suggest that the world shown is one in which the harmony, happiness and vitality shown in The Sun are terribly absent.

Sufi teaching seems to be that the development of those in whom the seed of spiritual growth is germinating takes them toward unity, through the *'alam al mithal,* or 'world of resemblances' or 'similitudes,' which itself is a projection of the Realities and the Names, which in turn emanate from the source of all being.

In The Moon – which is our world under the influence of the moon – nothing resembles anything: and, ultimately, nothing *is.*

A medieval Persian Sufi and religious thinker named Jurjani wrote that all spirits are either in light or in darkness, and that while the ones who are ignorant become even worse, spirits who are enlightened improve by following a path of suffering. Perhaps the very absence of human figures in the scene in The Moon is an indication that, insofar as 'self' is the barrier, as it were, what is represented is meant to be a subjective condition and, as such, one still in flux, not yet decided, and not without hope. It is not, after all, certain that there is no one inside that ruined tower. In the Hell shown on The Devil card, by contrast, all hope is lost: there, Jurjani's 'bad' has gone not only to 'worse,' but to 'worst.'

The Arabic *'adam* means 'non-being' or 'nothing'; and much use is made in Sufi literature of the implications of this for its other status as the name of the first man. *Ghair* means 'other.' From one point of view, God being all, there is no 'other,' and no 'nothing': Sufi authors have said that *'adam* (non-entity) is what is beyond what God created, and that what seems to us to be evil either consists of relationships among dissonant *asma* (names), or it arises from *'adam.*

God, says Sheikh Ibrahim Gazur i Ilahi, becomes his own *ghair* by veiling himself from himself, condemns himself, and flees himself, thus becoming the Hopeless One (*Iblis*), and meriting the name 'Satan.'

Figure 22. Shamash, the sun god, rising between two mountains.

If part of Figure 22 looks familiar, that is because it contains, of course, Figure 14.

It is a lion on the left, not a wolf or dog, and a goat on the right. It is surely obvious how the remarkably square and even mountains between which Shamash rises have become the two towers in the Moon card; and, dare one say, it is even apparent how the mysterious shapes at the bottom of the card image derive from the shapes in the pattern in the seal impression that, presumably, represent the rocky earth. Whether someone knowingly transformed the personified sun into the round moon with a face in it will almost certainly never be known.

Arabic for 'moon' is *qamr*; although another possibility for its source here is *shahr*, similar in sound to a word for 'sun.' *Ghamr*, however, is a word for 'flood,' and may be the more likely origin in view of one of the best known Mesopotamian myths.

The Persians also used cylinder seals; one of theirs is shown in Figure 23. The sun-disk was not only a symbol of the sun god in pre-Persian Mesopotamian religion; the Persians also used it

Figure 23. Persian cylinder seal showing two scorpion men with a sun-disk. Louvre.

for their supreme god – Ahura Mazda – because they identified him with the sun. Ahura Mazda was a supreme deity, creator and ruler, who yet found it necessary to create a number of subordinate gods, the Amesha Spentas, or Mighty Immortals.

Mythology is full of beings of a composite nature: probably the most familiar is the centaur of the Greeks. The disconcerting creatures in this Persian seal impression are scorpion men; that is, they have the upper torso and arms of a man, and the lower body of a scorpion. Not very nice at all, and Gilgamesh didn't think so either when he wanted to get past them.

Yet Gilgamesh himself was not Persian. Whether this means the graves of scorpion men of more than one nationality will someday be found is impossible to say. Gilgamesh is, as well as can be ascertained, a historical figure, and was the king of the Sumerian city of Uruk in the first quarter of the third millennium BCE. The poem describing his search for a solution to the problem of human mortality, *The Epic of Gilgamesh,* is probably the single most famous piece of literature of its degree of antiquity, and many see in it the forerunner of, for instance, Homer's *Odyssey.* Very briefly, Gilgamesh, who also happened to be two-thirds god, early in his career tended to take advantage of his status and make free with his city's resources, including its women, and also liked to fight, for which he preferred the men.

A sort of Tarzan or Sasquatch figure, a wild man named Enkidu, who lived with the beasts of the field and knew nothing of civilization or culture, and who ate grass with gazelles, came along and had a wrestling match with Gilgamesh, which

Gilgamesh won, and after which they became best friends. Gilgamesh cheated, however, because he first sent a prostitute from the Temple of Ishtar to have her way with Enkidu, something that apparently took six days and seven nights. When it was finally over, Enkidu found that the animals did not want to know him anymore, so he asked the prostitute to introduce him to the nearest place with an exciting downtown scene, which was Uruk; so she did.

Gilgamesh and Enkidu have various exploits, including the vanquishing of the monster Humbaba with some help from Shamash. Ishtar the Love Goddess is so impressed by this that she makes a certain suggestion to Gilgamesh; but he, noting the tendency her lovers have of coming to sticky ends, says, 'Thanks, but no thanks.' Ishtar further expresses her point of view by sending plagues and other misfortunes to Uruk. One of these is the Bull of Heaven, which the two friends slay, in turn causing no little commotion in the world of the gods, with the consequence that Enlil strikes Enkidu with a fatal illness.

After Enkidu dies, the distraught Gilgamesh sets out on a quest to reach the wise Utnapishtim, the Sumerian Noah, and the only human survivor of the Great Flood, who was, with his wife, granted eternal life at the source of the rivers, far beyond the habitation or, indeed, the venturing of any other human.

Gilgamesh meets the fearsome scorpion men at the edge of the world. They guard the frontier there, and try to talk him out of proceeding further. He would not have been Gilgamesh had he not continued, of course; and once he has passed the scorpion men, he has a series of otherworldly experiences with the sort of people you don't meet walking in the mall, and undergoes ordeals and tests and, ultimately, successfully crosses the waters of death to where Utnapishtim and his wife live. In reply to Gilgamesh's question as to how immortality is to be attained, Utnapishtim tells him the story of the Flood, and especially of the interesting relationship he had with Ea, the god of the water and of wisdom, who warned him and instructed him in how to prepare. Gilgamesh finally returns home after other educative experiences, which would seem superficially to be about the importance of paying attention, administered by the wise Utnapishtim.

Variations exist in the telling, according to place and era. It seems likely that it contains information on more than one level and, as so often seems to be a stumbling block with such things, part of the problem is that our tendency to insist on uniformity and consistency precludes the flexibility and intuition needed to grasp that the parameters of the context for interpretation may shift unpredictably.

In his initial general behavior, Gilgamesh obviously represents the commanding self or, possibly, even the *nafs al haywaniya*, the 'animal self,' to which regular commanding-self people may sink if they are not careful. He meets and does battle with his 'twin' – Enkidu, the wild man – which is to say, unconditioned or less-conditioned reality, a spiritual reality that is also his own real self or, possibly, a teaching pertaining to it. Enkidu is rendered presentable after his rendezvous with and seduction by Ishtar's agent, which represents the capturing and relative neutralizing of that reality by the lower, conditioned world. (Another ancient story with the same theme is the Biblical story of Esau and Jacob.) Enkidu's struggle with Gilgamesh may thus also correspond with the manifestation of the accusing self, and their subsequent harmonization with the inspired self, or *nafs al malhama*: Gilgamesh and Enkidu together slay Humbaba, the beast in the forest; as it happens, another spelling of *malhama* means 'bloody combat, slaughter.' Gilgamesh rejects Ishtar's offer to give him a status like that of Dumuzi – who now spends half of every year in the underworld as a consequence of his association with her: this may, analogically, indicate a rejection of the counterfeit version of something real. As his punishment, Ishtar sends the Bull of Heaven after him; but the 'punishment' may actually represent a kind of reward when you consider that Sufi teachers like Ghazali sometimes describe certain spiritual states as 'like falling into the clutches of a ferocious beast.' 'A wise man is bound to fear a tiger. God said to David, 'Fear me as you fear a tiger.'' The 'slaying' of such a 'beast,' too, may represent a positive resolution, because it in turn has another inspiring consequence; or, it may mean a failure in the sense that the energy sent down was somehow nullified.

The death of Enkidu reminds Gilgamesh of his own inevitable passing. In the allegorical context, if the slaying of the Bull of Heaven indicates a refusal of a difficult aspect or stage of learning, it makes perfect sense for Enkidu to likewise disappear, since he represents the experience of the spiritual reality. If the 'death' that flummoxes Gilgamesh really represents the death of the spiritual seeker's ability to continue on the path, then the spiritual state represented by the Bull of Heaven may be equivalent to an infusion of precisely that energy needed to enable further seeking.

Utnapishtim himself very much resembles the archetypal Ancient Sage, corresponding in Sufi philosophy with the Universal Intelligence that is the source of all other archetypes. In that sense, this stage of Gilgamesh's journey evidences its explicitly metaphysical character, and suggests that the other events that have occurred are allegorizations of the stages leading up to it, which, therefore, must have been positively completed.

Any interpretation of the events in the Gilgamesh story will, surely, reflect the predisposition of, and the information available to, the interpreter: not, in fact, unlike the Tarot cards in some ways.

Figure 24 shows Gilgamesh wrestling a lion; Figure 25 shows another figure, a deity, in a similar motif; and Figure 26 shows the Tarot card Strength.

Figure 24. Akkad period cylinder seal showing a hero subduing lion. Hirmer Verlag, Munich.

Figure 25. Detail of Akkad period cylinder seal showing a god slaying a bull. British Museum.

Figure 26. Tarot. Strength.

Contest scenes featuring curly-bearded fellows wrestling lions and apparently winning are yet another extremely common theme in the cylinder seals. In some cases, they are definitely identifiable as representations of Gilgamesh; and, sometimes, there is another chap there who looks like he is probably Enkidu.

The Strength card from the Tarot shows a woman who is either closing or opening the mouth of an animal that, in most cases, is obviously meant to be a lion. Whereas with Gilgamesh one is bound to wonder whether what one is looking at is a demonstration of sheer superior physical force, and whether that is, as it seems reasonable to assume, attributable to his being part god, when it is a woman one is inclined to think there is something else going on.

For those able to entertain the possibility, a miraculous dimension has often been associated with individuals of sanctity (however one understands that term); and that is not even to touch on the whole question of whether, as seems to be the case, there are many things ordinary people would be capable of had they not been told they weren't. The role of miracles among the Sufis has already been referred to. One historical Sufi saint in particular, however – Najm ad din Kubra (Great Star of the Faith) – was famous for his rapport with animals. A contemporary recorded how, when Najm ad din stood at the threshold of his *khanaqa* (meeting place), a dog that trotted by and came within his sight was transformed in a way paralleling the absorption of a mystic, and other dogs subsequently surrounded it and placed their paws onto its paw before going off to remain nearby but at a respectful distance.

Another fascinating passage that may shed some light on the significance of 'strength' in the scheme of things – or of things as they really are, and not as we think them to be – is from a book by a Sufi named Kashifi written at the beginning of the sixteenth century CE.

In it Kashifi describes how, as a youth, he spent a great deal of time in Herat, in what is now Afghanistan, in the company of a Sufi master named Saiduddin Kashgari. One day they were out for a walk, and came across a gathering of people watching a wrestling match. They decided to test their 'powers of the will' by first helping one of the combatants, and then the other. They concentrated together on the one they wanted to help, and he immediately gained the upper hand, subduing his opponent. Then they turned their attention to the other, with the same result. In this way – without, of course, anyone else knowing or suspecting what they were doing – they controlled the contest.

Kashifi then goes on to relate how, on another occasion, he and Saiduddin, in the company of two others with similar powers, encountered another such assembly watching another contest, this time one clearly unequal: one of the fighters, he says, was powerful, the other thin and weak. The stronger one, inevitably, was winning, and Kashifi suggested that they aid the weaker one as they had done before, by the 'power of (their) wills'; and by that means, concentrating on him, they enabled the thin and weak man to throw the much stronger one to the ground, turn him over and hold him down, much to the pleasure of the crowd. 'Of all those present,' Kashifi says, 'we were the only ones who knew the real cause.'

One of the best known sayings of Mohammed was, 'He is strong who controls himself when angry.'

A clue to the nature of a possible connection between strength and justice is given with rare clarity in a statement attributed to this same Saiduddin Kashgari. 'He claimed to be able to affect the minds of sovereigns in such a manner as to compel them to conform to his will, and even to leave their thrones and seek refuge at his feet. This power is called *tashkir*, or the 'subduing faculty.' The Shaikh says of himself:

'Were I to live as a Shaikh, none other would have any *murids* or disciples; but my business is to preserve Mussulmans from the evils of oppression. On this account I am in conflict with sovereigns, and must therefore compel them to conform to my demands, and so promote the welfare and interests of the true believers. Through the especial favour of the Most High, a strength or power is given to me by which, should I desire it, the Sovereign of Khatai, who assumes to be a god, would obey a letter from me, and, leaving his kingdom, come barefooted after forsaking his kingdom, and seek the sill of my door.

'Although I possess so much power, I am wholly submissive to the will of the Most High; and whenever it is a matter referring to the will, His command reaches me, and it assumes a bodily form. For this, great moral sentiment is essential, and it is this which subdues my will to the superior one of the Most High, so that it is His will which ensures justice.'[12]

The way to Strength was through Gilgamesh, the scorpion men, and The Moon.

As already noted, there was a Mesopotamian deity who corresponded with the moon in the thinking of the Sumerians and their successors, and his name was Nanna or Sin. Figure 27 shows him.

Figure 28 shows The King or Emperor from the Tarot.

If anything, in the Tarot's Major Arcana there are so many seated figures representing one kind of power or another that it becomes a question of trying to determine what, if anything, distinguishes any of them. Broadly speaking, there is the division into worldly and spiritual, and then, within those, division into

Figure 27. The moon god Nanna, from a Third Ur Dynasty (2050 to 1950 BCE) stele. University Museum of the University of Philadelphia.

male and female. Since, too, it is a set of symbols being dealt with, even where earthly dominion is explicitly shown the question is unavoidable of what kind of power, precisely (again, even taking 'power' in its broadest sense, to include other features that presumably go with rulership, such as wisdom and judgment), is meant when it is a matter of divining the truth of a situation that may have everything to do with something else and nothing, noticeably, to do with monarchs.

In other words, it is about qualities; which, in their status as qualities – rather than things that partake of the quality of grossness and, thereby, obviousness – are elusive. Recognizing this and acknowledging the difficulty of it may be the beginning of the development of the quality

Figure 28. Tarot. The King.

of wisdom, which would mean that the Tarot has already helped us in this undertaking, even before The Hierophant, or The High Priestess, or The Hermit have been reached.

Perhaps by the time we do reach them, we will be able to recognize them because they recognize themselves in us, or to the extent that they do.

Exactly how Mesopotamian kings were seen in relation to the gods appears to have varied over time. They were never quite thought of as deities in their own right, as, evidently, were the Egyptian pharaohs. Moreover, there were kings of cities, and those cities had their own gods, so that the cities were not all of the same status, just as there were hierarchical relationships among those gods. The great lawgiver Hammurabi of Babylon is described in an inscription of the time as speaking of Anu and Enlil calling him 'to endow the populace with beneficence, I, Hammurabi, the dutiful and god-fearing lord, to imbue the land with goodness, to extirpate evil and wickedness, so that the weak will not be harmed by the strong, and that like the sun I will rise, illuminating the land, over the black-headed folk.'

The king was, thus, an intermediary between the world of the gods and the world of humans and, in this respect, he – like the magician, but with a different emphasis – resembled a priest.

Energy is not the only concept for which a meaningful context has only relatively recently developed; others include evolution and consciousness. The evaporation of a literal understanding of 'God' and 'Creation' was largely a result of the assimilation of a number of empirical observations and their assembly into Darwin's Theory of Evolution. It is a matter of puzzlement to some that many appear oblivious to the fact that it is nonsensical without reference to ideas (such as natural selection, 'select' being a transitive verb and, thus, one that requires a subject) that are no less abstract and metaphysical than the idea of a deity: the religion of science, a cult as blind to its own cultishness as any other.

The Sufi idea of evolution of individual consciousness may have some connection with the theme of evolution of the whole of humanity, but the nature of that connection inevitably remains a matter for speculation. The Book of Genesis contains a passage that some read as an explicit reference in mythological language to a process resembling the one experienced by the many level headed and, sometimes, traumatized people throughout the world who report having been reluctant guests of powerful humanoid beings who tap these individuals' biological resources in order to produce new beings that are, as they are being called by researchers in this area, hybrids. The possibility cannot be excluded that what has been assumed to have been the natural (whatever that means) process of human evolution has really been the result of massive covert intervention on the part of higher intelligences, whereby they introduce into our population individuals who are the product of this hybridization: physically inconspicuous, but carrying significantly more genetic material from the above-human source than does humanity as currently constituted. There are allusions, too, in Sufi writings that make sense when it is assumed that an extraterrestrial liaison is somehow involved.

The literature about Rumi, for instance, includes *Manaqib al 'Arifin*, (*Qualities of the Wise*); one of the narratives in it describes how Rumi, at the age of 16, was in the habit of leaving, by night, the school in what is now Aleppo where he was studying. An official, wanting to know what Rumi did on these journeys, followed him one night to beyond the city walls and to the Tomb of Abraham (at Urfa, now Sanliurfa), where he saw 'a domed structure...filled with strange men,' who met Rumi. It says that they were men 'unlike any he (the official) had ever seen before.' The poor man passed out from fear and, when he recovered, there was no sign of the structure with the dome or the 'strange men.'

The superiority or 'kingliness' that the Sufi is believed to have realized is that of his having become a 'completed human being,' or *insan al kamil*, which is even the title of an important text by Jili.

In one historical Sufi metaphysical scheme, the downward emanations from the highest level of being consist of six stages or worlds. Between the first and the second stages comes the first thing created, variously called the 'First Intelligence,' the 'Pen,' or the 'Reality of Mohammed' (*haqiqa al muhammad*), which is the mirror in which God is able to see his own attributes. The third world is the world of souls, the fourth the world of similitudes, the fifth is the external world and the sixth is the *insan al kamil*: so called because he includes in himself all divine attributes and Names. He is also, thus, the fulfilment of the Reality of Mohammed.

Another way of looking at it is that there are four technical terms that use the word 'man': *al insan al kabir*, the Great Man, or Macrocosm; *al insan as saghir*, the Small Man, or Microcosm; *al insan al kamil*; and *al insan al hayawani*, or Animal Man. Men (meaning humans, of course) are born as *al insan as saghir*. They can rise to become *al insan al kamil* – or they can sink and become *al insan al hayawani*.

The common Arabic word for 'king' is *malik*, which can also mean 'angel.' Just as there are numerous words for 'strength' in both Arabic and English, so the terms denoting rulership are many. 'There are but two beings,' wrote Ibn al 'Arabi, 'who may rightfully call themselves 'God.' One is God, who, in His revealed Books, calls Himself Allah; the other is the Completed Man' (*al 'abd al kamil* – *'abd* actually means 'servant', so it is 'Completed Servant'). Another term sometimes employed in this respect is *al khalifa Allah*, 'vice-regent of God.'

There is, therefore, the king as the servant of God or the gods and, also, of the people, whether or not his discharge of these functions accompanies his attainment of a spiritual station or his inheritance of a temporal one. (There is also a spiritual 'king,' who is not only not likely to be a temporal ruler, but is likely to flee such involvement, if historical examples are anything to go by.)

Yet we also have the king as tyrant, as bad guy; as destroyer, not servant, of the people; as object lesson in what *not* to do to please the gods, rather than as the person closest to them. If it is true that the Tarot cards have much to do with Sufi teaching, it may be justified to consider this aspect of kingship as well and, above all, its manifestation in the microcosm of the individual human being.

The Sufi idea, as already mentioned, is that the self in which most of us are stuck most of the time is the *nafs al ammara*, or commanding self, and the terms in which it has been described have depended, inevitably, on the understanding and vocabulary available to the cultures in which the teaching of which it is a part have been expressed.

Figure 29. Detail of mid-ninth century BCE stele showing Nabuplaiddin (not shown) being presented to Shamash. British Museum.

The seated figure on the right in Figure 29, which is more of the same stele shown in Figures 11 and 12, bears a remarkable resemblance to the moon god, and with good reason; because it is another representation, an artistically more developed one than in Figure 14, of the sun god, Shamash. Again, what is shown is not the whole image, but only as much as the artist who produced Figure 30 used.

The sun-disk of the god has become a turning wheel; the supplicant on the left has become whatever that human or half human figure plunging down the wheel on the left

Figure 30. Tarot. Wheel of Fortune.

75

is supposed to be; one of the rampant lions on the side of the stool on which the god sits has become the creature on the up-swing. One of the curious waist-up-only beings leaning out from the front of the canopy over Shamash's shrine has become the bizarre individual on the top of the wheel: although it looks as though elements of the god himself may also be present. The table under the sun-disk, too, has become the support for the wheel.

The complete scene is shown in Figure 31.

Figure 31. Nabuplaiddin being presented to Shamash enthroned in his shrine.

What can possibly be made of The Wheel of Fortune in the context of everything discussed so far?

The most obvious meaning, taking it on its own, is the frankly banal one that 'things change.' What else is new. Beyond this the idea is reducible, perhaps, to the notion of change itself. It is axiomatic in most religious thinking, let alone esoteric depths, that the life of man is one of change and decay: everything living is born and must die; and if there is a realm beyond, it is there, and nowhere else, that the painful cycles are escaped.

A belief in a transcendent reality, whether or not born out of painful experiences in this one, more often than not makes unavoidable a belief in rewards and punishments, causes and effects; and, indeed, the notion of *karma* is now a familiar one even in our culture, at least to the extent that even if someone doesn't know exactly what it means, they have almost certainly heard the word. The religious cultures that gave us the word and the idea also maintain the possibility of escape from the cycle of suffering, over the course of many lifetimes: Hindus call it *moksha*, and Buddhists, of course, *nirvana*. The aim is not to get to the top of the wheel, but to get off the wheel altogether.

In Sufi literature are to be found allusions to hidden patterns in ordinary life; and sometimes there are also implications that while man as he is may be misguided about and have an understanding that is at best partial of whatever good and evil may be, there are, nevertheless, realities corresponding to the ideas of merit or lack of it, and also of punishment and reward. Rumi even states explicitly (in his discourses): 'Although God has assured that good and evil will be rewarded on the day of resurrection, it is also the case that every moment brings with it a foretaste of what is to come then. If a man should feel happy, it is a reward for having made someone else happy. If he is sad, it is the consequence of his having caused another to feel the same. Such things are bestowals from the other world, and representative samples of the day of judgement, and an opportunity for one to come to some understanding of these important subjects, in much the same way that corn in the hand may be presented as an indication of the heap...You should realize, then, that forlornness and bad moods and ill tempers such as you experience are the result of your having committed some sin and inflicted some hurt. Even though you don't remember precisely what you did, the nature of the payback should be enough to tell you that you have been responsible for much evil. Nor do you know whether those evils were deliberate or inadvertent...'

It may be worth noting too that while for the cultures that

gave us the word *karma* reincarnation is a given and, for Islam, with which the word 'Sufi' has historically been associated, it is not, it is the contention of the teaching being considered in relation to the Tarot that in addition to having been transmitted by the Prophet Mohammed, it has also existed since before recorded history, and is the inner aspect of all authentic religions, including those that do encompass a belief in multiple and successive earthly lives.

It is also a fact that reincarnation is an important article in the beliefs of certain religious groups in the Middle East that are considered heretical by orthodox Muslims of both the Sunni and Shia persuasions – examples are the Ahl-e Haqq of Turkey, the Druse of Lebanon and the Yezidis of Iraq; and it is true that each of those groups originated in the teaching of a Sufi sheikh.

Mention has already been made of Gurdjieff and his disconcerting ideas about the moon. In the second book from his own hand, *Meetings With Remarkable Men*, he relates in storytelling fashion various adventures he and his fellow seekers had, and describes journeys they undertook and some slightly Gilgamesh-like things that happened to them. (He even tells of hearing verses from the epic as a child, with the clear inference that he did so within the context of a tradition directly transmitted from ancient times.) It is difficult to see how anyone can read that book without, at some point, grasping that Gurdjieff is – at least a good deal of the time – not describing things that really happened, but telling instructive tales. Sometimes they are allegories, and sometimes one simply will not be able to fathom what he is talking about unless one is already familiar with other sources. He made no secret, among those who later published accounts of him, of the fact that he was going to quite a lot of trouble to conceal his true meanings as well as he could.

In one passage, he informs the reader of his intention of describing in detail a certain part of a journey that he made with his colleagues in the area of the Amudarya River in Central Asia, and of doing so in a manner approximating the style of a certain school of literature that he had, as chance would have it, studied when he was still a youth, and that also just happened to have arisen and thrived on the shores of that very river: and that the name of the style in question could be translated as something along the lines of creating images without recourse to the use of words.

There is here an allusion, first, to the fact that to get all that one can out of the book in which the passage appears, one has no choice but to consider assessing graphically descriptive sections as themselves constituting references to data not explicitly given: a big clue to this is the absurdity of a literary technique that doesn't use words. Second, perhaps, it is a nod in the direction of the Naqshbandi Sufis, so named after Bahauddin Naqshband, a Sufi master of the fourteenth century. The word *naqsh* is Arabic for 'diagram' or 'painting,' and the name 'Naqshbandi' is thus often translated as 'Painters.'

It is worth looking again at the image of Shamash sitting receiving Nabuplaiddin, and considering in juxtaposition to it another passage in *Meetings With Remarkable Men*.

In the passage in question, Gurdjieff is describing what was ostensibly an attempt he made to relieve his poverty by setting himself up as a shoe shiner on a public street. Not having much luck at first, he decided he needed to innovate, and so obtained an armchair of some special kind, and put one of Edison's phonographs underneath it, where it would not be seen by casual observers. To this he connected, he says, a flexible tube with, on the other end, an apparatus that the customer, while resting comfortably in the armchair, could put to his ears even as Gurdjieff surreptitiously started up the record player for them. He even names the *Marseillaise* as one of the pieces of music they would indulge in (others being operatic works) while he shined their shoes. Further, he says, he affixed to one of the arms of the chair a tray to bear liquid refreshments and magazines. He notes that his advanced ideas about customer service paid off well.

A third passage may be reflected upon in the light of the two odd bearded figures, who only seem to exist from the waist up, leaning out from the front of the covering of Shamash's shrine in Figure 29 or 31.

He says that, one day, as he was walking on the Kurfurstendamm (in Berlin) toward the Zoological Gardens, he spied a man, who had lost both of his legs, on a little hand-operated wagon and turning the crank on an 'antediluvian' musical box. Somewhat further on, he again mentions the character, having related a story about his life as it had been before he came to his current predicament; again he describes him as without legs, operating the music box in the manner described, and accepting German coins of small denomination from passersby.

In the book, and also in conversations, Gurdjieff referred to an ancient esoteric society called the Sarmoun Brotherhood. He says that it was founded in Babylon, and claims to have discovered and gained admittance to their then-extant manifestation somewhere in the Hindu Kush mountains of Afghanistan. He seems to be saying that this was a turning point, if not *the* turning point, in his search for knowledge.

Why should Gurdjieff and a society that is supposed to have been in existence for more than four thousand years be of any interest in the context of The Wheel of Fortune?

Gurdjieff incorporated into his teaching a symbol he called the

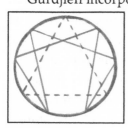

Figure 32. The enneagram.

enneagram (Figure 32), which more recent Sufi sources have affirmed originated with the Sarmoun, although they call it an enneagon, which would, presumably, be a figure with nine sides.

As Gurdjieff presented it, it is circular, is divided by nine equidistant points connected internally by straight lines, and is an expression in visual terms of the interaction of the 'law of seven' with the 'law of three.'

The law of seven and the law of three are also components of the teaching he apparently was attempting to prosecute. They concern, respectively: the tendency of any process to deviate from its original intention – it corresponds closely with the musical octave, wherein, at those stages where intervals occur, a deviation takes place, unless new force fills the gap; and the necessity for the presence of three forces – positive, negative, and reconciling – for any phenomenon to occur. Knowledge of these laws may be helpful in pursuing the mode of personal development that Gurdjieff sought to promulgate, because they govern that process no less than every other: although it might be said that the very purpose of knowing them is to be able to avoid their negative consequences, including by understanding that the working of the law of seven in this world means that every process, insofar as it partakes of the mechanical nature of our 'abode of decay,' eventually comes to fulfil the opposite of the intention with which it was started.

In recent years the man in the street, if he has come across the enneagram, is likely to have done so as part of the incredibly popular 'personality types' movement. There are believed to be nine principal types, and the manner of their interaction, and the paths for 'development,' from one type to another, follow the lines connecting the points on the circumference of the enneagram; which, in the authentic enneagram teaching as well as here, are thought to be in motion. (An enneagram that is not in motion, Gurdjieff said, is 'dead.') Although virtually every book on the 'personalities enneagram' announces that the symbol is thought to have 'originated with the Sufis' and was first made known in the West by Gurdjieff, they generally neglect to mention that there is no convincing evidence that the use to which they are trying to put it is a correct one, nor, indeed, that their approach has anything to do with anyone born before

Fatty Arbuckle tried the Prison Diet.

In discussing the concept of the commanding self, the question inevitably arises of whether, or to what extent, modern Western culture is based on it, with, for instance, its ubiquitous narcissism...

Then again, too, acclaimed French film director Francois Truffaut evidently considered *Invasion of the Body Snatchers* (1956) one of the greatest films ever made. It is unclear, though, whether he was thinking of the Hollywood version that is the one everyone has seen, or the original, which concluded with the small-town doctor stumbling about the busy highway and shouting hysterically and futilely, trying to warn anyone who would listen that humans were being killed and replaced by articulate vegetable replicas.

One word for 'wheel' in Arabic is *bakra*, which, as *bikr*, means 'maiden,' like the figure in The Star. Another is *daulab*, close to *daul*, meaning 'destiny,' 'turn,' 'vicissitude,' and also, for that matter, 'empire, dominion, sovereignty,' and 'good fortune'; *duwala* is 'misfortune, calamity'; *dalal* is a 'broker, auctioneer, public crier': it is conceivable that the figure in The Magician was meant to be something like this. *Dala'* means 'strength,' in the sense of 'endurance, perseverance.'

The word *buruj*, as already shown, means not only 'tower' but, also, 'signs of the zodiac.' The signs of the zodiac, more often than not, are, or include, animals. A word for 'heaven' or 'firmament' (also 'sign') is *sama'*; *ism*, on the other hand, with the same consonants, is 'name' or 'noun,' as in 'Names of God.' (One might also proceed from 'noun' to 'thing' and the 'realities.') 'These,' wrote Shah Waliullah, 'are the Names (Attributes) of God, ever in cyclical movement. He who is guided to understand this cyclical chain of movement along with its predications is certainly guided to all good.'[13]

The reference in The Wheel of Fortune may simply be to celestial, what some would call astrological, influences in general. If so, we are up against a wall – or, perhaps, like the people of Babel, on top of our tower, but still not able to read the mind that arranged the stars, physicists who claim a Unified Field Theory is just around the corner notwithstanding...

The crux of the matter where destiny, whether inflicted by the stars, or by genes, or by accident, is concerned is concisely expressed by the Sufi Khirqani: 'The people of the world receive what is in their book of destiny; the spiritually evolved receive something else in addition.' Khirqani's formulation does not, however, raise, much less answer, the question of whether the transcendent nature of the extra-destiny influences means that there are, or are not, destinies that preclude their receipt; were that not the case, perhaps, the 'spiritually evolved' would be everyone, and the notion of destiny itself would be without meaning.

Figure 33. Hammurabi's Law Code Stele, circa 1700 BCE, showing Hammurabi in Babylonian prayer position before Shamash, the sun god and god of justice. Louvre.

Shamash turns up again at the top of a famous artifact known as the Law Code Stele of Hammurabi. His

declaration about himself and how he saw his job as king has already been quoted. In Figure 33, we see him face to face with the god to whom he reported.

Justice is also a Tarot card (Figure 35),

(Figure 34. Detail of Amorite (1830 to 1350 BCE) cylinder seal showing Ishtar. Pierpont Morgan Library, New York.)

**Figure 35. Tarot.
Justice.**

and Figure 34 is an example of one of many cylinder seal impressions from which the image may be derived. Here is less certain ground, simply because there are so many images similar to this one, and some of the seated figures in the cards look as though they could be based on any of them, or on more than one. Ishtar here dangles a scimitar that seems to have morphed into the scales of justice, and holds a mace that has become a sword, just as the arrows in the quiver peeking over her shoulder have sprouted into what are, presumably, the wings of the Justice lady.

Quite a number of Sufi stories suggest intricate interrelationships among forms of justice, including something like a subtler justice in the ordinary world that happens in ways one would never expect and, also, at an understanding of justice with regard to personal evolution that is, again, quite different from the other kinds.

The classic example is surely the story, first appearing in the Koran (Sura 18) but retold often since, of the meeting between Moses and a mysterious individual, called by God himself 'one of Our servants' and one to whom he had 'taught knowledge': traditionally taken to be Khidr, the unseen and immortal guide of the Sufis. Moses begs Khidr to allow him to accompany him and learn from him. He succeeds in persuading Khidr to let him try to do so, but finds that Khidr's actions seem so outrageously unjust that he cannot refrain from challenging him about them, even though it was part of the deal that he would not do so. Khidr eventually dismisses Moses, and reveals to him that his actions were just in the sense that they were to a greater good than Moses, with his ordinary perception, had been able to grasp.

A word similar in sound to an Arabic word for 'wheel' and

that means 'justice' is *'adl*: it carries connotations of 'equity, honesty, uprightness, making equal.' Another word for 'justice' is *qist*, with a narrower emphasis on 'right measurement.' The primary word for 'balance,' such as the figure in the card holds, is *mizan*.

The Koran contains references to 'the Balance' as a gift from God to man. Sura 57, 'Iron,' says: 'We sent aforetimes our apostles with Clear Signs and sent down with them the Book and the Balance, that men may stand forth in justice; and We sent down Iron, in which is mighty war, as well as many benefits for mankind, that God may test who it is that will help, unseen, Him and His apostles.'

'Book' is *kitab*; a homonym is *qutub*, literally 'pole' or 'axis,' and the name for the hidden chief of the Sufis, on whom the very continued existence of the material world is said to depend. *Mazn* (after 'balance') means 'manner, custom, usage' (as in 'way' or 'path'), and also 'state, condition,' and 'sudden departure, flight': the Sufi *hal* is spoken of as a 'gift' that descends without warning, and the Sufi is sometimes called 'son of the time' or 'moment.' An alternate meaning of *hadid*, iron, is 'of quick understanding, of fluent speech'; *hadd*, further, means 'goal, aim; reach, sphere of action; definition, rule; edge, point; strength, bravery; manner, way.' *Hadd*, with a different Arabic letter *d*, is 'stimulate, spur on, investigate'; *hadd* with a different *h* means 'liberal, generous, magnanimous,' and *hada'*, 'halt, stop, abide' (as in 'stage'); *hadi* is 'conduct, way of life,' and 'be rightly guided, find the right way.' Loud resonances of Sufi themes are obviously present among these meanings.

An example of a Sufi occupying a certain role in a complex and, perhaps, ironic interaction between fulfilment of the *shari'ah*, or religious law of Islam, and something construable as extralegal justice may be the story of Sadrudin, the oldest son of Bahaudin Zakariya, reported to have been the Sahrawardi Sufi who did more than any to spread that order in India in the thirteenth century CE. When he inherited enormous wealth from his father, he gave it all to the poor, citing his own failure to share Zakariya's immunity to the corruption all too likely to be wrought by such luxury. 'The following incident, which is recorded by the historian Farishta, has often been quoted by Muslim writers as one of the saint's miracles. Muhammad Shah, eldest son of the reigning king Balban, was Governor of Multan, and had married the granddaughter of the late king Altamash. She was a very beautiful woman and her husband was deeply in love with her. Once, however, in the state of intoxication he divorced her 'irrevocably' i.e. by thrice uttering the words signifying separation. On recovering his senses he was deeply grieved to learn what he had done, for, according to the Muslim law, the only way he could take her back as his wife, was for her to be regularly married to another and then once more be divorced.

'The Qadi of Multan suggested to the Governor that Sadru'd-Din, who stood in high repute as a saint, be asked to act as an intermediate husband by marrying her for one night only. As the

Governor was most anxious to receive her back as his wife he agreed to the proposal. The records state, however, that on the following morning Sadru'd-Din, at the request of the bride herself, refused to give her up. The Governor was so enraged at this that he made the plans to put the saint to death on the next day. But it so happened that in the night Mongols besieged the city of Multan, and during the course of the day, the Governor fell in the fight with the invaders. This incident is regarded by the saint's biographers as the direct intervention of God

Figure 36. Detail from Akkad period cylinder seal showing Inanna bearing weapons and on a throne decorated with lions. Private collection.

thereby justifying his retention of the Governor's wife.'[14]

More seated women, and more Ishtar.

The feminine aspect of sovereignty: an additional complexity to the already many-sided matter of kingship.

Figure 37. Tarot.

If it means anything, it may mean exactly that merciful side to justice; which is to speak of what it may represent, and not to offer a sentimental view of women as 'nicer' than men.

The Empress.

It may mean 'mother nature,' as distinct from 'father god.'

It may mean something like what was represented by the woman who was the real mother of the baby in the well known story about King Solomon, in 1 Kings, Chapter 3, verses 16 to 28. There were two women in a house; they both had babies, and one rolled over onto hers in the night, and killed it: so she took the other's. They quarreled over whose baby it was until Solomon ordered a sword to be brought, and the baby cut in two, and half given to each woman. The real mother, appalled, relinquished the neonate, but the pretender quickly agreed to the slicing scenario.

That the human brain comprises two hemispheres, with a division in specialization of functions between them, is now so well known as to be almost part of popular culture. In broad terms, the left brain performs linear and sequential, logical and analytical functions: to which processes of division are essential. The right brain deals with simultaneity, spatiality, creativity and processes dealing with wholes. Recent discoveries indicate that the brain is more flexible than might have been assumed, so that in cases of injury, for instance, some adaptation can be made to compensate for losses; but the general duality is a fact nonetheless.

The story about Solomon describes the difference succinctly and, the more one reflects on the story in this light, the more dimensions are revealed: it may even give us clues about how the two sides interact. It challenges us, if nothing else, to consider the significance of the baby itself, and how it finishes up with the correct mother through Solomon's uncovering of the false one.

Consider the mothers' respective responses to Solomon's challenge. The real mother, representing right-brain mentation, for which there is no separation of observer from observed, but only 'the experience,' acts selflessly, and succeeds in preserving the baby. The false mother, symbolizing the reductive, analytical approach to things, the one that seeks to understand everything by dividing it up into ever-smaller pieces, acts with an absolute selfishness that would, without Solomon's intervention, result in the destruction of the very thing she purports to love. Hers – because the first division made is the one between self and object, observer and observed – is the mind that says, '*I* am having this experience, *I* will have to see what *I think about* it.' She seeks to split the atom, and succeeds in threatening to split the world.

What does this tell us about the respective roles of these two basic sides to consciousness in the context of the development of the individual and, even, about their potential importance for the survival of the human race? What does Solomon himself represent, in his role of administrator of the test and overrider of the wishes of the false mother?

The rather staggering implication is that whoever thought up the story (which is clearly symbolic, since it makes no sense at all for the false mother to agree to seeing the real baby halved, especially when she has gone to so much trouble to get it in the first place) knew something about the brain and its workings that our scientists only arrived at a few years ago.

Insofar, moreover, as the mind may be said to be 'sovereign,' and the real mother in the story to have herself exercised sublime judgment, it may not be far wrong to consider it an example of what The Empress signifies – the female traditionally representing the passive, and every level, as pointed out, being passive in relation to the one above it. In the story, she becomes something like a queen when Solomon, the king, defers to her.

A further description of the interrelationship of the two poles of mental activity and, perhaps, how they connect with something beyond – in other words, how our spiritual life, or potential spiritual life, becomes our psychological life – is in the story of Esau and Jacob in the Book of Genesis.

The two are born as twins, Esau the elder, to Isaac and Rebekah. While still pregnant with them, Rebekah feels them 'fighting' and, when she asks God why, he tells her that 'the younger will be the stronger,' and 'the older will be his servant'. Esau is born 'covered in red hair'; as they emerge, Jacob 'grabs his brother's heel.' Esau becomes an outdoorsman and hunter, and Jacob 'settles down' and becomes 'a shepherd.' Jacob gains Esau's birthright one day when Esau comes home so weak with hunger that he is near death and requests some of the 'red stew' (other translations give it as 'pottage') Jacob is cooking, and Jacob demands his birthright as the price. After consuming the food, Esau gets up and leaves, as if nothing significant has occurred. Jacob later completes his usurpation of Esau's rights when Isaac, old and blind, is dying, and asks Esau to kill some wild game to prepare some of 'that tasty food that I love so much' before giving him his blessing. When Esau has gone to hunt, Rebekah, who favors Jacob, coaches him in the deception whereby he, Jacob, kills some of his goats and puts the hairy hide on his hands and neck while she makes a meal from the meat. Jacob then proceeds to successfully impersonate Esau, even though Isaac notices the difference in the voice, and obtains the blessing meant for Esau that will mean sovereignty, prosperity and fertility. When the deception is discovered, Isaac sorrowfully tells Esau that he has no further blessing to give; and he adds, 'You will live by the power of your sword and be your brother's slave, but when you decide to be free, you will break loose.' (It is curious that, while Esau, as should not surprise us, vows bloody vengeance, references to their subsequent relationship evidence none of these elements.)

Esau, like Enkidu, is that part of the human being that has an affinity with 'the wild': in other words, 'higher' and relatively unconditioned reality. 'Hair' in Arabic is *sha'ir*, a homonym of *sirr*, 'secret'; and *hamr*, 'red' – it also means 'to flay, skin' and 'grow stupid, like an ass' (or like the right brain, if you ask the left brain) – is susceptible to having its consonantal sounds rearranged into *haram*, 'sacred, forbidden, unapproachable' (and from which we get the word 'harem,' of course).

'Heel' is *'aqb*, which also means 'what follows immediately,' and also 'son, offspring, progeny'; *'iqba(t)* means 'sediment, dregs' (the coarse element that is Jacob's province). *'Akb* is 'nimble, alert, brisk,' as the calculating left brain seems when compared with the right brain. *Kabb* means 'overthrow,' as Jacob does to Esau, and as our own ratiocinative and egocentric minds do to our finer faculties all the time; *khabb* is 'deceit, treachery'; *khub(at)* is 'hunger,' the weakness that represents the comparatively delicate nature of what the right brain does. *Khaib* means to be 'excluded, expelled, deluded in one's hope, disappointed.' *Ghaib* means to 'conceal', 'secret, mystery, obscure,' and, especially, 'being absorbed by the contemplation of transcendental things – mysticism.'

The word for 'grab,' 'seize and hold,' is *qabad*: further meanings are 'close the hand and make a fist,' 'take possession,' and 'usurpation.'

Wasu'a (after 'Esau', of course), on the other hand, corresponds to meanings of 'spacious, vast, extensive,' 'contain, comprehend, encompass, include,' and 'be generous, liberal, open-handed': suggestive of the spatial, 'holistic' (to use an overused word), and selfless aspect of the mind. *Waswas* is 'temptation, delusion, fixed idea,' and also 'anxiety, concern, melancholy.' *Iswa* means 'example, model, pattern.'

Among words associated with the idea of 'stew' or 'pottage' are *saliq(at)*, which means 'what is boiled, cooked, kitchen herbs,' but also 'custom, usage'. Esau is 'raw', Jacob is 'cooked'; what happens, the basic dilemma, is that the 'raw,' the real and unconditioned, falls prey to 'custom and usage,' and loses its 'birthright.' It is a 'red' stew because, like the reality Esau represents, it is 'forbidden' in the sense of being 'holy' to the more conditioned world, and also because, once it arrives in that world, it appears 'stupid' to its denizens.

It is, then, Esau's nature not to understand deception, cunning, or ambition; he has nothing to do with them, so he is not impressed by the fact that he has just lost something that he didn't know how to value in the first place (as indicated by his thinking that his birthright wouldn't do him much good if he was dead from the hunger he was experiencing). The stew thus represents the mixing-together of higher and lower realities, in which the higher, or finer, is overwhelmed by the lower and coarser. In that sense, too, it is 'forbidden' to Esau; his not being able to live unless he consumes it is a way of saying that pure, unmixed higher reality cannot subsist in its pure state in our world: it has to take on some form, some disguise that, from the point of view of its more perfect origin, also amounts to a defect. It might also represent the attempt of the conditioned, left-brain dweller to attract as much of the higher reality as he can in order to try and make use of it.

The root of the word *haram*, arrived at through applying the time honored and widely employed method of rearranging the consonants (of *hamr*, 'red'), has, in addition to its broadest meaning of 'forbidden, holy, sacred,' other associations that are instructive in the context, some of which are contiguous to the main one. For instance, it also means 'deprive, dispossess, divest,' 'take away, withdraw, withhold,' 'deny, refuse,' and 'exclude, cut off' (all of which may, obviously, be said to apply to what Jacob does to Esau).

The idea of something being proscribed, of course, applies, paradoxically, to both that which is forbidden because it is holy and to things considered taboo through being just the opposite. In the context of the meaning of the story, it might be said that the sacred reality that is the reason for earthly mechanisms like religion coming into being is the same reality that those same mechanisms very quickly find a threat to their continuing existence and, thus, hasten to condemn. Jacob in the story can also be seen as either the analytical mind with too much power taking advantage of the holistically-oriented right brain, or as the individual who is aware he is in that predicament attempting to experience the higher dimensions to which his right brain may give access.

Further rearrangement of those sounds gives us *mahir*, meaning 'skilled, expert, practiced, experienced,' continuing the theme of the importance of the idea of conditioning, of the freshness of reality being deadened through use.

(Isaac may also have been senile (*haram*), and while the kinship (*rahim*) of Esau and Jacob did not result in Jacob showing Esau any kindness (*rahmat*) when Esau was at his mercy (*marhamat*), Esau wept (*hamr*) on discovering that Jacob had, in effect, held him to ransom (*mahr*)...)

Isaac in his fatally weakened condition represents the same reality as Esau rendered delicate by extreme hunger, the same hunger that Isaac now expresses when he states his desire for some of Esau's strongly flavored wild game (the vividness of less-conditioned reality). The difference is this: Esau, after partaking of Jacob's bowl of stew, recovered; Isaac is not going to recover. Sufis say that spiritual states are temporary, but stages are permanent. From this point of view, the story is an allegory of progress, and Jacob impersonating Esau represents not deception, but emulation. A homonym, *maz*, of 'goat,' *ma'az*, means 'insipid, tasteless': recall Sahrawardi on love of the essential seeing depths and degrees within a quality, rather than a quality in contrast with its opposite. *Mu'zam* means 'principal, most important, best quality or sort,' and *maiz*, 'priority, prerogative,' such as Isaac gives to Jacob.

Sufi teaching itself is said by some to have been superseded through the ages — many sheikhs abrogated practices and instituted new ones – primarily because of the very theme being considered, of the corrupting nature of the conditioned world: and insofar as it has related to religious dispensations, Ibn al 'Arabi, distinguishing between kinds and degrees of prophethood, even went so far as to say, in his *Futuhat*, that prophethood 'will continue until the Day of Resurrection. It is not possible for information coming from God or knowledge of the universe He created to do other than continue. Were they to cease, that universe could no longer receive the nourishment it requires to continue to exist.' Moreover, the Arabic word for 'inheritance', *tarika*, sounds very similar to *tariqa*, 'way' or 'path,' a term commonly used by Sufis for their own activity.

Isaac tells Esau he will 'live by the power of (his) sword'. Arabic for 'sword' is *saif*. Yet another extrapolation of the *haram* root, *hiram*, means 'a woolen blanket worn over the head and upper body': and the primary Arabic word for 'wool', of course, is *suf* (pronounced 'soof').

The implications may also be considered of Esau being 'older' or 'preceding' and of Jacob 'following immediately' and 'grabbing' Esau's 'heel.' The reality that Esau personifies is timeless, like the simultaneity of right brain experience, contrasted with the sequential, linear and temporal nature of the left brain and 'this world'; the image of the two infants 'appearing' suddenly in this manner, with Isaac grabbing the heel, suggests the spontaneity and immediacy of thinking itself: as if every thought we have that we recognize as a thought (and to the extent that we are aware of it, to the extent that we are aware of a 'we,' a subject – like the hand closing into a fist – it is a left brain phenomenon) bears some relation to something else (what might, for lack of a better term, be called some other kind of 'thought') analogous to the relationship between Jacob and Esau at their birth.

That the importance of the duality of consciousness that in our time has found an anatomical correlative in the brain hemispheres was something recognized by the ancients is further shown by the fact that the Jacob and Esau story is far from being the only part of the Jewish scriptures to deal with it. It has been said that much so-called sacred literature is really a record of technical knowledge in an unfamiliar form. The story in Numbers of Balaam and his donkey is surely an exceedingly strange one, but its strangeness becomes incidental when it is read for what it is: an elucidation of certain aspects of the difference between the two modes of mental activity.

King Balak of Moab calls upon 'Balaam son of Beor,' whoever he was, and asks him to come and place a curse on the Israelites, who have grown 'huge' and settled near him. During the night God tells Balaam that the Israelites are on his (God's) side – or he is on their side, whichever way you want to look at it – so he, Balaam, shouldn't curse them. After further urgings from Balak, God tells Balaam he can go with Balak's representatives, as long as Balaam does what God tells him.

Balaam sets out on his donkey with two of his servants, on the road to Moab.

Inexplicably in view of the permission he has just given, God 'was angry that Balaam had gone, so one of the Lord's angels stood in the road to stop him. When Balaam's donkey saw the angel standing there with a sword, it walked off the road and into an open field. Balaam had to beat the donkey to get it back on the road.

'Then the angel stood between two vineyards, in a narrow path with a stone wall on each side. When the donkey saw the angel, it walked so close to one of the walls that Balaam's foot scraped against the wall. Balaam beat the donkey again.

'The angel moved once more and stood in a spot so narrow that there was no room for the donkey to go around. So it just lay down. Balaam lost his temper, then picked up a stick and smacked the donkey.'

God then inspires the donkey to speak to Balaam, inviting him to wonder why it was behaving the way it had been: whereupon Balaam is allowed to see the angel blocking the way. The angel rebukes Balaam for going to Moab, and points out that if the donkey had not stopped, he would have killed Balaam, and spared the beast.

The donkey wandering off the road and into the open field is the intuitive, nonsequential, spatially oriented right hemisphere at work. The narrow path with a stone wall on each side is the focused and orderly left brain. The donkey lying down when its way is utterly blocked is a figurative representation of the fact that, by its very nature, the left brain's parameters are limited. Examination of the Arabic words for 'foot,' 'wall,' and 'scrape' reveals a range of meanings the most consistent feature of which seems to be their contradictoriness, referring especially to ideas of precedence and conclusion, limitation and bravery, representation and secrecy, pain and pleasure, worthiness and loss of honor through violating the rules, measure and estimate.

Further, though, the angel itself represents the spiritual reality that initially is visible to, and acts upon, the innocent donkey in each of us; and the beating of the donkey, the efforts and discipline of the individual, all to the purpose of gaining fuller vision of that same reality. Some support for such a view may be found when one discovers that *'air,* 'wild ass,' relating to a complex of meanings that includes 'roam about, wander,' also takes us to *ru',* meaning 'heart, mind, soul,' associated with meanings of 'frighten, startle.' Another, similar sounding, range of words includes meanings of 'see, perceive, know' and, also, 'become prudent, intelligent, wise and, by contrast, look foolish or stupid.' *Khadash*, moreover, a word for 'scrape,' sounds not only like *kadish*, 'cart horse,' but also *qadas*, 'holy.'

Developing that approach to the Balaam story, one may see the donkey's initial act of wandering into the field as, perhaps, representing an altered state, such as dervishes are said to experience, consequent to its vision of the angel. On being returned to the mundane world, the individual feels the pain of separation all the more keenly. In such an interpretation, the donkey's refusal to attempt to continue may be seen as indicating what in Sufism appears to be considered a kind of exhaustion of the false self of the seeker, coinciding with his new found ability to see the angel, the transcendent reality.

It is all interesting enough, of course; but one may get the impression that the right brain, as it were, gets all the good tunes. Are there any other stories in the Hebrew Bible that at once give insight into how the right brain mind works, and what may be a description of an inadvisable approach to relating to its activity?

Later in this book there will be reason to examine some material from the second book of Samuel. Another brief – only three sentences in the *Contemporary English Version* – interjection in that document reads as follows: 'Saul's son Jonathan had a son named Mephibosheth, who had not been able to walk since five years old. It happened when someone from Jezreel told his nurse that Saul and Jonathan had died. She hurried off with the boy in her arms, but he fell and injured his legs.'

The King James Version gives it as, 'when the tidings came of Saul and Jonathan out of Jezreel.'

Let us be clear about what happened, or is supposed to have happened, in this – again – undeniably curious sequence of events. Or is it, rather, simply the fact that someone considered it, for some reason, important enough to record in such a context that is curious? Either way: Saul and Jonathan had died.

Did they, though? *We* know that they did, because we have the preceding verses, which tell us they did. How, on the other hand, did Mephibosheth's nurse apprehend the intelligence? Was she there? Did she see it happen? No. 'Someone from Jezreel' *told* her. It is an allusion to the indirect, indefinite, intangible (by comparison with the left brain) nature of the life of the right hemisphere.

How does she receive the rumor? As if it is, on the contrary, direct, definite and tangible. She does not stoop, or rise, to the task of interpretation; she does not make the contribution from within herself that is necessary to be able to deal with it as it really is and for what it really is. She mistakes it for something else; just as people have been doing, for instance, with the Bible for a very long time.

She takes it as solid, simple, straightforward, easily understandable, scientific news, and tries to 'use' it as such, hurrying off with the baby because she draws the 'logical conclusion' that it means that the same thing will happen to him as happened to, first, his grandfather and then his father, and that that is the best way to make sure it doesn't.

She thinks it means she is supposed to run.

In doing so, she succeeds, on the contrary, in seeing to it that the very child whose welfare she is anxious to preserve will, himself, never, in fact, run – or even walk – in his entire life. The limited and limiting nature of the left brain descends with horrible immediacy, as if in vengeance at the usurpation of its legitimate sphere of functioning.

Or is the vengeance that of the intuitive realm, for the squandering (through what amounts to an attempt at illegitimately exploiting it) of its gift?

Thus, the author of this startling kernel of knowledge seems to be telling us, are some of the complexities of the very same mind each one of us is born with, the one we assume we already understand, and some of the perils of not using it correctly, and the urgency of learning to do precisely that.

Ishtar is shown yet again in Figures 38 and 40. In the first –

Figure 38. Detail of cylinder seal showing Ishtar beside the rising Shamash, with water-streams containing fish emanating from Ea (partly shown).

just off-camera, as it were – is the god of water and wisdom, Enki or Ea. The objects Ishtar holds in Figure 40 are thought to be lightning or thunderbolts: partly because it is Enlil, god of the storm (among much else), that she and her lion are towing in his chariot. It is anyone's guess which of these or similar seal images went into producing the Tarot picture of the woman in Temperance pouring from one vessel into another. It is such a far cry from the meaningful content of most of the Mesopotamian images considered thus far to anything like what is implied by the word 'temperance' that

Figure 39. Tarot. Temperance.

one has to assume that the real intention, in the context of whatever wisdom the card images were meant to impart, of this card is at least *something* to do with the word.

It may be as interesting, though, to consider the implications of the image. Who knows? Juxtaposing them with the words may be even better.

A being that is evidently an angel pours some liquid from one vessel into another. Let us call the angel a 'he.'

Is the liquid a beverage? Is he measuring out how much may be drunk?

Figure 40. Detail from Babylonian cylinder seal showing naked Ishtar on a fire-breathing winged lion, yoked to the chariot of Enlil (not shown). Pierpont Morgan Library.

What sort of beverage would an angel be pouring?

If it is not something to be drunk, what is the significance of the liquid?

What is one of the most significant characteristics of liquids, in a relative if not in a literal, scientific sense, that may be said to constitute their symbolic property?

Is it not formlessness? What does not have form? That which is not matter. What is not matter?

In order for the act of pouring to occur, what is required of the two vessels? Must they not be on different levels? One higher, and one lower?

Does this imply that the substance poured, the energy, the mind, the whatever, becomes different in the act of pouring?

Or does it imply that the energy that originates on a higher level descends to a lower level, and inhabits a different form, without in itself being changed?

One of the best known metaphysical systems that purports to give a comprehensive explanation of reality, including its origin and man's place in it, is the Kabbalah, which is a large body of teaching – more diverse than most of its contemporary students, probably, realize – that is almost without exception identified as of Jewish origin, although even within that assumption opinions differ as to whether it dates from the time of Moses, or from even before that or, rather, from medieval Europe.

In *Origins of the Kabbalah*, Gershom Scholem describes the problem of the Kabbalah's origin and the initial phases of its development as second only to the subject of the destruction of the Second Temple in its importance for the history of Judaism. By no means, he asserts, have the source materials received adequate attention, and he indicates that a reason for that is that they are all but bereft of material that can be thought of as historical in the sense of shedding any light on those origins or their circumstances.

The symbol with which the Kabbalah is most widely

associated is the one sometimes called the Tree of Life, which consists of ten words, representing powers, essences, archetypes, or aspects of divinity called *sefiroth*, linked diagrammatically by straight lines. According to some interpretations, they are to be seen as simultaneous emanations of the infinite; in others, as successive and interdependent ones. Indeed, according to an old edition of *The Jewish Encyclopedia*, the original Kabbalah did not even have ten *sefiroth*: it had eight, and came from a Muslim group known as 'The Faithful Brothers of Basra.'

The Faithful Brothers of Basra were the *Ikhwan as Safa*, the 'Sincere Brethren,' a group of Ismaili (a Shiah subgroup) Muslims whose tenth century CE work was their *Rasa'il (Letters)*, an encyclopedic undertaking that attempted to make available the knowledge of the time, including what we would call esoteric or metaphysical knowledge. They considered themselves heirs to the most ancient wisdom of Pythagoras and Hermes, which the Sufis also say is identical with their tradition.

The same *Jewish Encyclopedia* tells us further that 'Eleazar of Worms' statement that a Babylonian scholar, Aaron B. Samuel by name, brought the mystic doctrine from Babylonia to Italy about the middle of the ninth century, has been found to be actually true... The fact is that when Jewish mystic lore came in contact with Arabic-Jewish philosophy, it appropriated those elements that appealed to it; this being especially the case with Gabirol's philosophy on account of its mystical character...

'The following doctrines of Arab philosophy especially influenced and modified Jewish mysticism, on account of the close relationship between the two. The 'Faithful Brothers of Basra,' as well as the Neoplatonic Aristotelians of the ninth century, have left their marks on the Cabala. The brotherhood taught, similarly to early Gnosticism, that God, the highest Being, exalted above all differences and contrasts, also surpassed everything corporeal and spiritual; hence, the world could only be explained by means of emanations. The graduated scale of emanations was as follows:

1. the creating spirit (*nous*); 2. the directing spirit, or the world-soul; 3. primal matter; 4. active nature, a power proceeding from the world-soul; 5. the abstract body, also called secondary matter; 6. the world of the spheres; 7. the elements of the sublunary world; and 8. the world of minerals, plants and animals composed of these elements. These eight form, together with God, the absolute One, who is in and with everything, the scale of the nine primal substances, corresponding to the nine primary numbers and the nine spheres. These nine numbers of the 'Faithful Brethren'...have been changed by a Jewish philosopher in the middle of the eleventh century into ten, by counting the four elements not as a unit, but as two.'[15]

(In another place, Blavatsky said that 'the three higher (*sefiroth*)...are supercosmic abstractions and *blinds*.'[16] How this squares with the presentation just given is not immediately apparent; but it will be.)

'The Cabala, however,' *The Jewish Encyclopedia* continues, 'is not a genuine product of the Provencal Jews; for just those circles in which it is found were averse to the study of philosophy. The essential portions of the Cabala must, on the contrary, have been carried to Provence from Babylon; being known only to a small circle until Aristotelianism began to prevail, when adherents of the speculative Cabala were forced to make their doctrine public.'[17]

Why should the Kabbalah be thought interesting in the context of the Tarot card Temperance?

One of the meanings of the Arabic word *qabala* is 'to receive' (as the lower vessel, the one being poured into, does). Some of the metaphorical language in which Kabbalists over the centuries have struggled to describe their understanding of the working of the *sefiroth* involves references to them as 'vessels' into which, and from which, one to another, a sublime reality or power is 'poured' from its celestial origin, and that each *sefirah* manifests in a different way in order to produce what we experience as the universe, including ourselves. In *Major Trends in Jewish Mysticism*, Scholem presents the familiar idea of the Tree of Life as one with many *sefirothic* branches but a single, unknowable root. The sap of the root, the concealed root of the root, and the transcendent reality beyond the *sefiroth* and the tree itself are the *En-Sof* (or *Ain Sof* or *Ein Sof*), usually translated as the 'absolutely infinite.' The Tree of Life is the cosmic skeleton; and everything, even the most trivial, that exists only does so through the potentiality bestowed on it by, and active through it from, the *sefiroth*.

More to the point as far as Temperance is concerned, within some strains of Kabbalistic thought it is axiomatic that the third (*Binah*) and last (*Malkuth*) *sefiroth* correlate to, respectively, etheric receptivity on an infinite scale, which is the way God reveals himself to himself, and concrete receptivity on a profound level, which is the substance of creation.

Where, if at all, might the name 'Temperance' come in?

Within the notion of temperance can easily be detected the ideas of control, of watchfulness, of vigilance: indeed, in most traditions of consciousness development, there is none without some form of watchfulness. Within historical Jewish mysticism – both, apparently, apart from the tradition of the Kabbalah and, at times and in some ways, confluent with it – are the teachings of the *merkabah* ('chariot') mystics. They were and are so called because they took as their point of departure the first chapter of the book of Ezekiel, wherein the prophet has his vision of God's throne: which, in motion, becomes a chariot. It was, says Scholem, nothing less than the earliest form of Jewish mysticism. Jewish mystical authors at various times spoke of an 'ascent to the *merkabah*,' in the sense that it is 'above' man's ordinary life, and also of a 'descent' to its vision, because it is also within his own being. It was a complex and hazardous journey of many stages, and preparation for it involved austerities, repetitions and physical postures, especially the head between the knees.

Even with such a broad sketch of the Kabbalistic *sefiroth* as we have given, their essential similarities with the 'throne-world,' in the sense that they are both ways of seeing the divine in the profane, or the divine behind the profane, are evident; and in discussing the seven lower *sefiroth* in the context of one of the earliest known Kabbalistic works, a book called *Bahir*, Scholem writes that a variety of symbolisms directly taken from the works of the *merkabah* mystics were, at that seminal stage, used to represent the seven lower *sefiroth*, thus infusing the Kabbalistic legacy for generations to come with those otherwise, strictly speaking, non-Kabbalistic elements.

There is, thus, a connection between the Kabbalah and the ideas of control, of discipline, of temperance. Indeed, an idea that runs throughout Kabbalistic literature is that the *sefirothic* Tree of Life is also a representation of man, and that man is the microcosm of the universe, which is the Body of God. By exercising watchfulness over himself – or at least, with that as a first step – man can attain the vision of the whole beyond himself. The similarity with Sufi teaching about the 'complete' or 'perfect' man is obvious.

Markabat is Arabic for a 'vehicle, carriage, beast for riding,' from the verb *rakaba*, 'to ride, drive, sail, make use of any vehicle.' The verb *raqaba*, spelled and sounding almost exactly the same, means 'to observe attentively, to be on the watch for, watch, expect, guard.'

The advisability of proceeding on the assumption that the significance of the Temperance card might have 'something to do with' the word notwithstanding, beyond the themes already examined there is not, unfortunately, enough information to make it possible to say exactly what that something is. It will be clear by now that the imagery of the Tarot, although its source has been identified, is to one degree or another obfuscated by the apparent incomprehension of the artist; the names of the images, likewise, while they may have been taken from literary material accompanying the source images, are not only not always assigned to the correctly related image but, in all likelihood, have also been garbled, perhaps seriously so, by an imperfect understanding of the language of that material. It seems likely that the graphic content has also been distorted in the direction of trying to make it correspond to the misinterpreted words. Thus, we may have a word or words applied to one (or more) images that really apply to another, or others.

In the case of Temperance, if the word is taken on its own, without considering it to be an allusion to a discipline of any mystical sort – it is the name of a 'virtue' and, as such (like it or not), when evaluated outside of a purely moralistic context, neither here nor there – there are at least three Arabic words any of which could have been the original; and on the premise that that word was itself a misreading of another Arabic word, there are so many candidates that there is no way of knowing which it was.

One of those words is *i'tidal*, meaning, in addition to 'temperance,' 'equilibrium between two things' (Justice). *Tadlal* means 'cry out for sale, sell by auction' (Magician); *tadallul*, 'be on friendly terms with' (Sun); *tadliya*, 'take in by deceit' (Magician); *tadawal*, 'circulate' (Wheel of Fortune). *Tadhayul* means 'walk proudly' (commanding self), and 'come down in the world' (Tower).

Another is *ta'fif*, from *'af* ('abstemiousness'). *'Atf* means 'turning' (Wheel). *Watf* means 'hang low' (Hanged Man).

Tawarra' is from *wara'* ('abstinence'). *Ithar* is 'vengeance, retribution' (Hanged Man). *Tar* means 'turn, time' (Wheel); *tartatur*, 'calamities' (Tower); *tarath*, 'inheritance' (like *tarik*, a homonym for *turuq*, which Idries Shah maintains is the source of the word 'Tarot' itself); *thaur*, 'bull' (Bull of Heaven); *tauriya*, 'cause to disappear, change by sleight of hand' (Magician).

We have to add a bit on to Figure 38.

Some think the lady with the bird feet in Figure 43 is Lilith,

Figure 41. Detail of cylinder seal showing, from left, an unidentified deity, Ishtar, Shamash rising between mountains, and Ea.

Adam's first wife.

Whether she is Ishtar or a more obscure out-of-the-ordinary woman, she is obviously striking in her resemblance to the Tarot's Devil. Add scepter raised aloft; add whatever those things are that bind what are apparently miniature devils – and what is the Devil doing keeping his own rank and file in the condition traditionally thought reserved for the human souls he has acquired? – from the other ancient images, such as the adjacent gods in Figure 41,

Figure 42. Tarot. The Devil.

which, again, are by no means unique, and it is even harder not to think that this is one of the things someone was trying to copy when they drew the picture that, ultimately, turned into the one

Figure 43. A clay plaque from Isin-Larsa, Old Babylonia period (2000 to 1600 BCE), showing a nude, winged and talon-footed female deity. Louvre.

Figure 44. Akkad period cylinder seal showing Ishtar with her lion before a lesser female deity. Oriental Institute, University of Chicago.

on this laminated card that could, as Blavatsky said, be purchased 'at almost every bookseller's in Paris.'

The beasts below the woman in Figure 43, like the chained devils in the card, have horns. Ishtar, in Figure 44, holds in each hand a long, straight, narrow object – in one, a leash for her lion, in the other, a mace – that can easily be seen turning into the chains that bind the devils by their necks.

There is the Devil of popular conception, derived from monotheistic religious teaching – the Hebrew religion, Christianity, Islam and, perhaps, Zoroastrianism. Insofar as we think about it at all, however, what we assume is simple about this subject turns out not to be at all: if the phrase 'the banality of evil,' for example, is accurate, it is surely a conundrum that Satan is the most interesting character in Milton's *Paradise Lost*.

With or without reference to a Devil, to be sure of what you think is evil, it probably helps to know what you think is good. The flag-draped villains of history have always seen themselves as heroes and saviors of their people, and sometimes of the rest of the world as well. Gurdjieff, too, put it very concisely when he said that for the vast majority, evil is an entirely subjective matter: whatever furthers the satisfaction of their desires is good, and whatever impedes it is evil for them. The divergence of desires among people in the collective thus, obviously, results in everyone doing what they think is good, and destroying each other in the process. There is, said Gurdjieff, absolutely zero chance that the human race, as currently constituted, will ever come to universal agreement about what is good. There is something like a real version of good and evil that can have meaning for man, he pointed out; but it is only possible in the context of wanting to achieve something real in the sense of evolving. Once that journey has been started on, whatever helps in it, just as in the subjective realm, is good, and whatever hinders it is bad.

Clearly, the issues surrounding the awakening of conscience (as discussed under The Star but with reference to Death and a myth about Enlil) and that of the commanding self (discussed under The King) have once again come to the fore. Herein is the practical significance of 'evil' and 'the Devil.' There is a continuum between this level of thinking about them and the more philosophical questions of how evil came to be in the first place if God is good and supremely powerful, and so on. In the tradition that tends to see all reality and all being as identifiable directly with God, evil itself is only possible as an absence of being, and not a positively existing force.

Yet, when asked whether or not there is some force that could be described as 'conscious' – which is to say, not dismissible as evil in the mechanical, subjective sense already discussed, and that actively opposes human conscious evolution – Gurdjieff answered with a qualified 'yes'; when pressed about the question of its nature and origin, he gave an explanation that he further qualified by saying that the full account was complicated, and of no immediate practical benefit to pursue. In his concise version, however, he introduced the term 'involutionary'; and his use of it may be illuminating in coming to some understanding of the meaning of 'evolutionary' and 'involutionary' processes in the context of the law of seven, one of the two universal and cosmic laws represented in the enneagram, understanding of which some Sufi sources in turn affirm to be of great importance. Commencing on the part of absolute reality (or 'the Absolute'), a process that is describable as involutionary becomes, at the next stage, less conscious and more mechanical, and becomes more so at every subsequent step. (The question is thus raised of what these 'steps' are; the answer would seem to be that they correspond to the notes of the descending octave in the law of seven.) A process that can be called evolutionary, on the other hand, is one that, on the contrary, begins with a modicum of consciousness, and develops in such a way, or in such a direction, that that degree of consciousness increases.

Here is where it becomes somewhat difficult. At certain points in the involutionary process, elements or, if you like, fragments of consciousness (whatever that may mean) from the evolutionary process somehow become factors in the involutionary process and, in that context, act in opposition to the evolutionary process itself. To the extent that they succeed in that enterprise, they even interfere with the evolutionary process, and cause its fragmentation and the separation of smaller evolutionary processes from the overall one. The separated fragments of consciousness that are now working against the development of consciousness in the larger context may even come together, and become parasitic, in the sense of living off the energy they drain from the larger evolutionary process by opposing it.

Keeping this idea in mind, let us consider the traditional Islamic explanation of the origin and nature of the Devil, who is usually called, in Arabic, *Iblis*:

'The devil is believed to be descended from Jann, the progenitor of the evil genii. He is said to have been named Azazil, and to have possessed authority over the animal and spirit kingdom. *But when God created Adam, the devil refused to prostrate before him, and he was therefore expelled from Eden.* The sentence of death was then pronounced upon Satan; but upon seeking a respite, he obtained it until the Day of Judgement, when he will be destroyed.' [My italics.][18]

The name 'Iblis,' again, means 'the wicked one,' or 'the hopeless.' His other name in Arabic, *Shaitan*, means 'one who opposes.'

Satan particularly disliked that he, a creature made of fire, was expected to humble himself before man, who was made of mere clay:

'So the angels prostrated themselves, all of them together: not so Iblis: he refused to be among those who prostrated themselves. God said: 'O Iblis! What is your reason for not being among those who prostrated themselves?' Iblis said: 'I am not one to prostrate myself to man, whom Thou didst create from sounding clay, from mud moulded into shape.' God said: 'Then get thee out from here; for thou art rejected, accursed. And the curse shall be on thee till the Day of Judgment.'' (Koran, Sura 15, verses 30 to 35.)

Gurdjieff's explanation as conveyed by Ouspensky is confusing inasmuch as he says that the broken-away pieces of consciousness that unite and are, in effect, evil in the sense that they oppose the (new) evolutionary manifestation are themselves from the evolutionary process (presumably an earlier, failed one), but that they do so at certain points in the *involutionary* process. The 'involutionary process' and 'evolutionary process' sound more than a little like the Sufis' 'arc of descent' and 'arc of ascent.' Apart from the context of individual souls, examples of involutionary processes would, one thinks, be all forms of higher teaching that become coarsened and distorted through progressively greater degrees of mixing with the lower levels of reality: like Esau eating his stew, or Ishtar in the underworld, or like a great religion twisted into a killing machine, or like Sufi teachings in a pack of cartoonish cards. The evolutionary process, however, would seem to be something that takes place partly through engaging with those remnants, if only to the purpose of developing the discernment to understand that that is what they are, and then going on to seek out fresher and purer impulses.

The idea of it happening at certain points in the involutionary process, then, can only mean when a certain quota of transcendent content has been lost; when a certain corner has been turned, in the sense of no longer merely deviating from the original direction, but becoming opposed to it. It resonates, like calling to like, with the errant consciousness at a vulnerable stage in its evolutionary climb, and turns it aside.

There is a parallel between the pre-existing Satan and the precedent nature of the evolutionary process that stops developing and gets cut off (Satan's refusal to follow orders), as there is between his becoming 'the hopeless one' (because he has stopped evolving) and 'the adversary,' and his opposition to further and new evolution – which, in the present context, happens to mean humans. His own process thus becomes an involutionary one.

The angels cannot be said to be either involutionary or evolutionary: they are what they are, and their 'prostrating themselves' before Adam is the demonstration of the completeness of their submission to God. The simplicity of their nature and the security of their station are not only not threatened by their humbling themselves before the new creature made 'of sounding clay,' but are proven by it. Here may be the answer to the question of whether Satan was an angel or a *jinn*. Angels are made of light, *jinn* of fire. In rebelling, Satan showed that he was not an angel: at least, not like the others; and the occasion and subject of his rebellion show that he may be thought of as a *jinn* who had, perhaps, reached a status almost like that of the angels, which is to say he was very highly evolved. But he failed a test of angelhood, the test of humility; and therein, of course, is the terrible irony. He lost what he wanted by wanting it. Had he been concerned with fulfilling the requirements for their own sake, the promotion would have happened, as it were, naturally.

Thus, also, are prophets opposed by the new owners of the religions of earlier prophets. The new evolutionary impulse always has to do battle with the decayed versions of the old ones.

If accounts both historical and contemporary are reliable, it would appear that *jinn* are more than figments of imagination.

In a book he wrote describing various people he had learned from, Ibn al 'Arabi told of a man of sanctity named 'Uryani who somehow managed to arouse the resentment of the other people in his neighborhood, in what is now Spain. One of the pillars of this community finally persuaded the others to expel him, and he went to stay with Ibn al 'Arabi's friends in Seville. As a punishment, Ibn al 'Arabi says, a *jinn*, or demon, turned up in the house of the individual who had incited the others to their ill treatment of 'Uryani. After forcing the owner out, the *jinn* summoned all the people, and when they came, proceeded to reveal to them – as a voice with an invisible source, evidently – all the nasty little secrets they were keeping from each other, who had stolen what from whom, who was sleeping with whose wife, and so on, referring them to evidence. This went on and on. They begged the *jinn* to leave, but it explained that they had brought it upon themselves by what they had done to 'Uryani, and insisted on staying for six months, continuing to expose their misdeeds even to their children and, generally, driving them all to despair. Finally, they could stand it no more, and went and found 'Uryani and begged his forgiveness. He returned, and the *jinn* left.

One of the ways the Devil, whether the Devil with a capital D is meant or just whatever level of devil you happen to have earned, seems to be characterized in Sufi material is something that is probably quite surprising to someone who has never thought of it that way. Like the snake whose form he took in Eden when he chatted-up Eve, he slithers silently, and can perform the most amazing contortions not only of physical movement, but of reasoning: when, for instance, rationalizing her into trying the apple.

Ghazali says explicitly that the nature of the Devil is to be found in the intellect perverted into service of the impulse to deceive for the further purpose of satisfying motives like greed, pride, anger and physical appetites.

Can The Devil be discussed without mentioning Hell? It is, after all, where he is supposed to hang his mortarboard.

Again, we have to make sure what we mean by Hell. If it is a bad place you might go after you die, it may have something to do with the *nafs al ammara*, inasmuch as it appears to be the commanding self that prevents the development that would preclude that occurrence or, at least, attenuate one's stay there. According to some Sufi authors, Hell has much to do with pride and self absorption: 'Be satisfied with yourself now,' wrote Sanai, 'and endure the hell of selfhood later.' The further equation of this condition with that of being unable to learn may have something to do with the Old Fellow being called 'the Hopeless One.' Ibn al 'Arabi appears to have encouraged this point of view when he wrote, in his often-translated *Fusus al Hikam* (*Jewel-facets of Wisdom*), that God's praiseworthiness is a matter of his fulfilling his promise of Paradise, and not of delivering on his threat of punishment.

Where the Mesopotamian Hell is concerned, the question of who was in charge may seem unimportant. As seen in the myth of Ishtar where she descended to the underworld, it was originally her sister, Ereshkigal, who ruled. Another myth, however, tells us that Nergal, the deity who presided over large-scale destruction, infiltrated the underworld, and placed his minions at its gates, all fourteen of them, and then dislodged Ereshkigal from her throne. She begged him to marry her and assume power, and he spared her. Inasmuch, on the other hand, as Nergal is that god of catastrophes, such as plague and war; and to the extent that such events are conspicuous examples of precisely that fate or destiny that spiritual development is said to be above and beyond; and inasmuch as that development, or lack of it, may have a direct bearing on one's situation after what is called death – far from being unimportant, the theme of a change of management in Hell may contain crucial information.

Where the Moon card showed a situation, a condition, in which there is no self to be seen and, yet, there is a suggestion of something that was, at some point, constructed, although it now may be in disrepair – the lunatic world, in which the fateful moon siphons off the energies that could, with effort, knowledge and luck, be raised to the spiritual level of the Sun; yet for which, paradoxically, there is still (in a word) hope – while that is the case with The Moon, the scene on The Devil may show the end result of persisting under that influence, of failing to escape it, where two beings regard each other with what may be desire, or loathing, or horror: but is unlikely to be indifference, because the fact that they are bound, held in stasis, would be meaningless if they had no will to be restrained and to make it worthy to be called Hell; if it is anything like attraction they feel, they are so similar-seeming as to make that something of a joke; and, if loathing or horror, the same applies, although for the opposite reason. They cannot even be said to have the satisfaction of being, fully, whatever it is they now are, as is demonstrated by their stunted state relative to the 'real' Devil who, obviously, rules over them, and of whom they – as a further dimension, almost a luxury, of unfulfilment – are prevented from seeing and knowing. The two may be and, indeed, probably are – in the perfect expression of the nature of Hell – the same person: and that person's being portrayed as two small, imprisoned devils may be the ultimate representation of what it means to have a self, to be a self, to be condemned to be that self, and never have the possibility of being anything but that self, yet not to know that self, and to *know* that you do not know yourself, and now never will.

Nor is it necessary, apparently, for physical death to have occurred for this situation to be realized: 'Many of those you see walking in the streets are really dead,' said Khirqani, 'and some of those who are in their graves are really alive.'

Figure 45. Detail of possibly north Syrian cylinder seal showing a nude goddess inside an arch motif with a bull and worshippers with a hawk and, apparently, a hooded cobra. British Museum.

It is now possible to see the myth of Ishtar's descent into the underworld, and liberation from it when Tammuz (Sumerian Dumuzi) the shepherd is procured as a replacement, as an allegory about the great laws that are also the subject of enneagram, and of other, 'sacred,' literature, such as the further stories from the second book of Samuel, to be examined later. The seven gates through which she passes are the seven notes of the descending octave, the octave of involution, that originates in a higher world, and results in the creation of our own. Ishtar's divesture alludes to the deterioration of the essential impulse of life with each stage, and her imprisonment and death, and the suspension of her corpse, to the emptiness of the intervals in the octave. The three greatest gods correspond to the three forces of

Figure 46. Tarot. The World.

the fundamental triad of creation that inhere in all phenomena: their intervention represents the filling-in of the intervals, which restores life to the branch of existence.

In terms of the particular context of the predicament of the human soul in the world, one of the Arabic words for 'substitute' also means 'ordinary, commonplace': the soul is lost in the 'ordinary' world, or the extraordinary (teaching) is made ordinary (and thus rendered ineffective). The 'dirt under the fingernails' (Arabic for 'fingernail' is *zufur*;

zafar means 'victory, triumph'; *zarf* is 'cleverness, resource-fulness; grace, charm,' and also the name of an element of grammar indicating place or time; *safar* means 'journey, travel,' and *sharaf* is 'honor, glory') from which Enki/Ea manufactures the creatures who revive her may allude to something of relatively little significance in a realm of greater understanding being of great potential value, and potential usefulness, to those in lower worlds, or to the 'remainder' idea discussed in the context of the Hebrew story of Lot, who also had an escape to make.

It has been speculated that the curved object that appears to enclose Ishtar, if it is her, in Figure 45 is a rainbow; but no one really knows. Nor is this the only such cylinder seal image. There are many like it. It looks, in fact, more like a rope.

It is common to interpret the four creatures in the corners of the World card as representing the cherubs that Ezekiel saw, and that turn up again in The Book of Revelation. The quaternity suggests the four elements, the four fixed zodiacal signs, and the points of the compass. The human, or humanlike, figure within the wreaths is sometimes interpreted as a woman, sometimes as androgynous, and sometimes as erect over water, whether standing or moving in some way.

Approaching these factors symbolically is obviously an exercise rich in possibilities. Especially in the context of the rest of the Major Arcana – and The World is traditionally placed last, or penultimate to The Fool, unless he is first – it may evoke the sense of a completion, a wholeness, achieved, a fruition attained after and consequent to the journey of and through the other cards and whatever they signify. Connecting it with the Almighty and the vision of Ezekiel obviously reinforces this idea, and facilitates raising the completion represented to a macrocosmic level; and many modern decks take this ball and run with it, renaming the card 'The Universe' or something along those lines. On the other hand, in a Tarot card reading, it could mean the completion of anything at all. The androgyny of the person in the middle, if that is what it is, can be taken the same way, as representing some sort of accomplished equilibrium. If it is not androgynous but, indeed, female, the inference is invited that her femaleness represents (as with The Star) a delicacy, a receptiveness, a yin and not a yang, a passive and not an active, a wise quiescence and not an agitated setting-out-on-new-undertakings; and if that isn't politically correct, recall that we are talking about symbols.

Ishtar had her lion, in the Mesopotamian religion the significance of which for all this has been under consideration, and the bull was Adad's, he being another version of Enlil. Birds have been noted and, also, plenty of other human-seeming figures who also rather looked as if they might have wings and were, apparently, interpreted by the original Tarot artist(s) as having them: even though they were, in the seal images, meant to be weapons carried on the back and protruding over the shoulders, or water-streams, or lightning, or other things easily mistaken for wings by someone trying to fathom these tiny, intricate portrayals of realities from cultures distant in space and even more so in time. It is not that surprising that the result should be something like what is shown in The World.

We cannot, again, know for certain that the process was indeed that haphazard; maybe it is the way it is because that is precisely the way someone who knew exactly what they wanted intended it to be. But even if that is the case, what *they* intended was not necessarily what someone even wiser, even older, also meant.

The Arabic word (*'alim*) that seems most likely to have been interpreted to mean 'the world' in the sense shown in the image on the card can also mean 'universe, kingdom, time, age, epoch, elements, creatures, men, people.' Alternative meanings are 'knowledge, learning; sign, mark, or pattern.' A different word altogether, *kull*, has the connotations of 'totality, the whole.'

The World Soul (*'alam al arwah*) and Great Soul (*ruh al 'azam*) are names given to a sphere of being in the hierarchical scheme of Sufi metaphysics. Yet other names for it include the Protected Slate or Preserved Tablet, and the Book. In an incomprehensible manner that is somehow neither creation nor emanation in any sense approximating the senses in which those words might be applied to the way in which subsequent levels – descents, as it were – of being come about, the highest, most sublime, utterly 'other,' beyond being and non-being, God, produced the Primal or Universal Intelligence (*'aql al kull*), the Exalted Pen (*qalam al a'ala*), the Reality of Mohammed (*haqiqa al muhammad*), the Mother of the Book (*umm al kitab*) – again, all different names for the same thing – and it was out of this level of being that the next one, the World Soul, was created. Further, the 'Realities,' the prototypes of everything in what we think of as the world, the particularizations of the Attributes or Names of God, were somehow transmitted through the Pen and inscribed in the Book, or World Soul, where they exist in a way that is outside of time and existence itself; and what we think of as the world is a partial and imperfect expression of them as mediated by levels of being in between.

All individual souls of human beings are one in the Great Soul. Rumi says, 'In the animal soul there is separation/ distinction, but the soul of humanity is one soul.' (Look again at the card.) It is the expression of God's own knowledge of his creation; all that is to happen is first written by the Exalted Pen on the Preserved Tablet.

Sometimes different levels of reality in this sense are, as already noted with reference to Shah Waliullah, referred to as angels; and it is said that this relationship, of active agent to passive medium, is repeated on all subsequent descending levels. In this sense, the lower the angel, the more its decree is subject to change; but there is no change in the decrees of the Exalted Pen.

Ibn al 'Arabi calls the contents of the World Soul *a'yan ath thabita* – 'latent realities,' or archetypes. They are the *muqtadayat* ('necessities' or 'inevitable consequences') of the Names and, also, the eternal essences of which the things in our world are the changeable existences. He even speaks of God 'clothing' them with existence, and seems to imply that these processes are to be understood as somehow evolutionary, in the sense that they occur in definite stages, even in time. These archetypes are the 'keys of the invisible' (*mafatih al ghayb*); while their relationship with the levels of reality above them – in other words, God, or absolute reality – is unknowable by anyone, the Sufi, Ibn al 'Arabi says, gains mystical knowledge of the archetypes themselves and of their relationship with our world.

The relationship of the World Soul or Tablet with the Universal Intelligence or Exalted Pen is sometimes compared to the one between Eve and Adam, the manner of generation of one from the other being analogous.

Something of the nature of the relationship between the 'realities' and 'remembrance' or 'mentioning,' in the sense of *dhikr* as practiced by flesh-and-blood people, may be gleaned from one of the traditions of Mohammed, retold in the *Ihya* of Ghazali, where he replied to a question about the nature of the gardens of Paradise by saying that they were the assemblies where *dhikr* was performed. 'The angels of God, all except the angels of creation, roam far and wide: when they discover an assembly of remembrance, they stop each other and say, 'Come, here is our purpose!' Then they all surround it, listen, and learn.'

The integration with the higher worlds that accompanies the attainment of the station of completion that is, from one point of view, the objective of Sufism appears to include some form of knowledge of these Realities and, thus, also brings new dimensions of responsibility for the Sufi when it comes to his relationship with the world he shares with us less developed ones. 'Only the sages and prophets,' says Shah Waliullah, 'have knowledge of the Tablets, through their 'taste' (*dhauq*).' Sometimes the same word – *dhikr* – is used to refer to the 'writing' of the 'Pen' on the 'Tablet' as to the activity of dervishes of rhythmically repeating the Divine Names; although they speak of this activity as 'remembering' (like, perhaps, the Platonic conception of learning; Waliullah said that in the higher worlds all cognition is 'recognition' or 'acknowledgement'), its literal meaning is more like 'mentioning.' Ibn al 'Arabi, again, wrote that not only does the individual consciousness in direct contact with the World Soul become like 'a pure, running stream in which all kinds of illuminated objects are reflected,' but the 'gnostic' (*'arif*) can, with his spiritual will (*himma*), cause changes in the world that would not otherwise occur; he himself was, like other Sufi masters, said to be able by this means to summon the spirits of Sufis from other eras and converse with them.

Ibn al 'Arabi's *muqtadayat* are certainly one kind of 'necessity'; but something of the range of necessities eminent Sufis are known to have not been above attending to may be felt if the foregoing is juxtaposed with the story about Abd al Qadir Jilani, in which a member of one of his vast audiences found himself distressed to the point of physical paralysis by his inability under the circumstances to satisfy a natural requirement. He concentrated on the Sufi and silently asked him to help. He reports that, as he watched, Jilani came down from the platform, while a duplicate of him remained and continued speaking to the crowd. The first Jilani approached the man and drew the sleeve of his garment across his head, whereupon the man found himself in a field with some trees and a stream; before relieving himself, he hung a bunch of keys he was carrying on one of the branches. Having concluded his prayers, the moment he had finished performing his ritual cleansing at the stream the man found himself back in the assembly, with his arms still wet from his ablutions, and Jilani still addressing the huge crowd.

Some time thereafter, the man found himself with his

Figure 47. Shamash rising and other deities.

caravan, fourteen days' journey away, when he came upon the same field: he found his keys still hanging from the branch where he had left them.

Figure 48. Tarot. Judgment.

We are nearly, but not quite, finished with the cylinder seal shown, in its entirety now, in Figure 47. The gods are truly proving themselves capable of taking on many shapes.

Where The World may superficially – and with the eternal nature of the World Soul in mind, perhaps, not so superficially – suggest completion in a somehow static sense, Judgment is often taken to indicate something like a resurrection, for reasons that are obvious. A resurrection, though, implies a death or destruction that has occurred and, in the context of the eschatological theme, a reckoning and, possibly, reward and punishment.

The image on the seal shows an assembly of major gods; which, in their capacity as planets, indicates, perhaps, some sort of celestial event. From the left, the one with the bow and arrow could be Enlil or, maybe, Nergal; then there is Ishtar; Shamash; Ea; and Usmu, Ea's two-faced attendant. Respectively, they correspond to Mars (if it is Nergal), Venus, and the Sun. It is unknown to which, if any, planets Enlil and Ea were considered to correspond; if the notion that peoples of extreme antiquity knew a great deal more than we usually give them credit for is to be taken seriously, it may be consistent to entertain the notion that they also knew more about the solar system than our own civilization did until quite recently. Then again, their attitude to celestial bodies was quite different from ours, and included what we would call astrology, although there is reason to think that their astrology was a more sophisticated affair than ours. Moreover, while some recent Sufis have indicated that while there is a science of celestial influences, meaning influences (whether they are called energies or something else) from the cosmos on life on this planet, including the life of humans, of which our establishment wise men are ignorant, it shouldn't be inferred that acknowledgement of such influences is a legitimate basis for abandonment of individual responsibility. Rather, if the ancient association of planetary influences with fate is recalled, it may help one to understand their relative significance, or insignificance, if one juxtaposes it with the assertion that spiritual development is precisely that which is outside of fate.

It may help us, too, to understand what is going on in this area if one takes into account the findings by some researchers (particularly, the late Michel Gauquelin) that the people who do show a clear correspondence between certain celestial configurations at the time of their birth and their field of activity, such as medicine and athletics, are those who are at the very forefront of those fields, and if one then connects that piece of information with the notion that the people who tend to excel in this highly visible manner also tend to be people with a strong personal essence: keeping in mind the idea that astrology has been said by some (Gurdjieff, for instance) to pertain only to an individual's essence, and not to his more superficial, and artificial, personality.

What is shown in the seal image is the sun rising, with other gods clustered around. In an astronomical or astrological sense this may, then, be speculated on as indicating some sort of conjunction. The Arabic word for 'conjunction' in this sense is *qaran*: it means 'close union, association, conjunction of the planets.' A related word is *qarin*, 'joined, yoked together, married; companion, partner; equal, ally; soul, self.'

In Islamic tradition, following the Koran and the traditions of the Prophet Mohammed, 'Judgment Day' – what is clearly meant by the 'Judgment' in the card – is *qiyamat* or *yaum ad din*. There are variations, such as *yaum al qiyamah*, 'Day of Standing Up,' and *yaum al bas*, 'Day of Awakening.' *Din* ('deen') thus means 'judgment' in this sense. *Yaum ad din* also sounds somewhat like a scrambled-up *indimam*, which is an alternative term for 'conjunction, meeting, collection.'

The rising of the sun may represent the coming forth of the purified human essence out of the dross of the other elements that together constituted the individual's unrefined and alloyed nature. In astrological and alchemical tradition, of course, the sun corresponds to gold, the manufacture of which out of base metals was the overt object of alchemy. It is fairly common knowledge among students of the subject that a major figure in the beginning of medieval European alchemy was Jabir ibn al Hayyan, the Sufi – known to the scholar monks of western Europe as Geber. Although a recognized transmitter of Sufi lore, he was not a Muslim, but a Sabaean; that is, he was an adherent of an ancient Babylonian soterial religion, or one the doctrines of which were expressed in terms of teachings about the stars and planets.

The purification, or transmutation, spoken of is allegorical of the process with which the perennial teachings about man's spiritual development, including Sufism, are concerned. Gold is incorruptible, and has other qualities that make it a suitable symbol for the best part of anything – including of the human being: the kernel, the soul, that will be shown in all its splendor, or lack of it, after physical death anyway. ('Coming Forth By Day' is even the proper title of the famous *Egyptian Book of the Dead*.) 'People are sleeping; when they die, they wake up,' goes another of Mohammed's most frequently quoted sayings; 'Die before you die.' Ghazali tells us over and over: 'This world is the seed-bed of the next.'

Indications exist in Sufi literature that their activity, the activity of pursuing *tasawwuf*, Sufism, in some ways partly depends on certain conditions prevailing on a higher level, which themselves wax and wane. Although crude astrology is forbidden by strict Islamic orthodoxy, one may wonder exactly how much to read into statements such as that of Ghazali when he says:

'There is a purpose for the existence of every star in the sky...The world is like a man, and everything in the world is like the organs of his body...You think that you are free to do anything you want, and that the unseen world has nothing to do with it. If you really believe that, you are like a child who sees puppets moving, and thinks they are wonderful because of the way they sit and stand and dance. All the time, though, the man who has made the puppets is behind the screen, where the child cannot see him, and it is he who is making them move. The wise man understands that the movements of the puppets are the work of the man behind the screen. To the wise, the people of the world are like puppets. They see the threads attached to them that no one else can see. Those threads are in the hands of the angels who move the heavens.'

The Ismaili (recall that the *Ikhwan as Safa* were an Ismaili group) mystic Nasir ad din Tusi described a hierarchical continuum of sequences of created beings wherein the highest aspect of each series is in touch with the lowest aspect of the next one above it, with the world of minerals at the bottom and the world of angels at the top, taking in, in descending order, the worlds of humanity, animals and plants. To any level in this hierarchy, the idea of paradise is represented by the level immediately above it: a point of view that also applies to the stages of growth of any one of the creatures within that level. The blindness of the newborn is hellish by comparison with the ability to experience the light that will be his in due course, and which is, consequently, paradisiacal for him while still not having opened his eyes; but by comparison with his still later ability to exercise the functions of maturity, such as movement and speech, it will be another hell for him. The independent spiritual incapacity of the ordinary adult to fathom the well known *hadith*, 'He who knows himself knows his Lord,' and so know spiritual reality, is hell for the walking and talking adult, and the attainment of that ability is, then, his paradise. Every stage is a taking off of one garb and the putting on of a new and better one, and as much a matter of acceptance as of active decision, so that it resembles an endless series of resurrections accompanied by engagement with new forms of spirit, the alternative to which is not stillness and stagnation, but reversion to a previous and hell-like stage.

On another level of allegory, the almost obtrusive multiplicity of figures collected around the figure of the sun god rising with his saw may be seen as alluding to the polarity of multiplicity and unity, separation and unification, that is fundamental to the Sufis' teachings on the science of spiritual 'states' and 'stations.' *Sharq* is 'east'; *sharaq* is 'split, cut in two'; and *shirk* is 'company, association, partnership.' *Sharq* also rhymes (another form of allusion) with *farq*, the root of *tafriqa*, the explicit term used by the Sufis for 'separation.' The opposite of these things is the state of union, *jam*, apparently meaning, on one level, in terms of re-integration of the individual's consciousness.

Reinforcement for this interpretation is found in the saw Shamash raises. 'To saw (apart)' is *nashar*, with associated meanings of 'announce, propagate, spread,' 'resurrect from the dead,' and 'be diffused, scattered, dispersed, thrown into disorder.'

The journey of the sun from east to west may thus additionally be seen as referring not only to a process that can occur to and within a person, but also, perhaps, to the way in which higher reality itself, or such teachings as make that process possible, are sent into this world, or how they are received when they are sent.

'West' is *gharb*, which also means 'pass away, depart, disappear; quickness, briskness; foreign country, exile; be bewildered.' To pass away or disappear is also the meaning of the Sufi term *fana*, applied to a spiritual state: states in general are said to appear quickly, suddenly, unexpectedly; the Sufi, moreover, is a foreigner in this world, and man is bewildered before the unfathomable reality he encounters when his status of being separated from it is dissolved and he disappears. Then again, when he does attain such a station, his condition is said to be near – the similar-sounding *qarb*.

Figure 49. Assyrian cylinder seal, circa 2340 to 2180 BCE, showing Zu before Ea. British Museum.

A priest and a priestess, and pictures of Ea, Lord of the Deep, the Wise, and the one who permitted the human race to survive by allowing Utnapishtim, the Sumerian Noah, to overhear him while he pretended to talk to the wall of Utnapishtim's house.

Current notions, in the West at any rate, of a priest are likely to be based on experience or observation of one form or another

**Figure 50. Tarot.
High Priestess/
Popess.**

of institutional Christianity. Jewish rabbis are certainly teachers, but are not considered intermediaries with the divine in quite the same way, nor are they usually thought to have the powers attributed to priests in terms of ability to definitively affect the supplicant's spiritual status. The teachings of Islam explicitly preclude a priesthood, mullahs and ayatollahs notwithstanding; and the *imam* was intended to be simply the one who leads the prayers in the mosque.

One Arabic term for 'priest,' with an emphasis on 'foretelling the future' or

Figure 51. Akkad period cylinder seal showing Ea enthroned in water with Shamash rising between mountains and ascending a ziggurat. British Museum.

'soothsaying,' is *kahin*. To 'predict' or 'prophesy' is *tanabu'*, from *nab'*; and *nabi* is a word for 'prophet,' as in 'the Prophet Mohammed.' Nebo or Nabu was the Babylonian god of writing, the equivalent of Thoth, Hermes and Mercury. *Na'ib* is 'substitute' or 'deputy.' As interesting, perhaps, is that the plural form of *na'ib*, *nub* ('noob'), means 'bee': the Sarmoun, of course, are known as The Bees.

Another word that means 'priest,' in a specifically Christian sense, is *qass*. It also means 'wish for, seek, aim at,' and 'suck the marrow out of a bone' – analogous to extracting the essence from events and materials. *Qaswa(t)* means 'be hard, rough, severe' (as the teacher may seem to the student), from *muqasat*, 'to endure, suffer, forbear with.' *Qash* is 'be well again after being ill' (being 'asleep' in the world is an abnormal condition), and *qasha'* is 'uncover, bare, take off' (as the seeker of knowledge must do, removing his layers of falsity and

Figure 52. Tarot. High Priest/ Hierophant/Pope.

conditioning). Among the meanings of a differently spelled word *qass* is 'impart, communicate, tell.'

The similar-sounding *ghass* means 'enter and travel through a country' (the dervish is instructed to travel, in the sense of exploring and coming to know himself), 'plunge or throw into the water' (analogous to use of learning materials), and 'find fault with, blame' (as in the accusing self).

A slightly tangential – or perhaps not – constellation of meanings is to be found in the word *'azm*, which can mean 'great, important, terrible': all of which may be considered to apply to a major aspect of the divine reality that a real priest, presumably, mediates or represents to humanity; or, 'beat or hit on the bones,' and 'give a bone (to a dog, for example) to eat.' The idea of a blow or an impact as a technique used in disciplining the lower self and producing a temporarily enhanced awareness – and perhaps the juxtaposition of this notion with that of extracting the marrow is itself instructive -- will be recognized by students of Zen Buddhism as well as of Sufism.

The days and nights as well of Mesopotamian priests were anything but badly planned, being filled with precisely timed prayers, liturgies and sacrifices, and with new moons and the ends of months marked by festivals. Each deity had its own priesthood, from the highest offices of (the Sumerian) *sanga* and *en* all the way down to the sacred temple prostitutes that scholars since the advent of Latin have politely referred to as 'hierodules,' very large numbers of whom, along with eunuchs, were necessary for the rites of Inanna/Ishtar to be properly performed. Speculation is still the best we can do when it comes to determining the precise functions of the various categories of priests, although their Sumerian and Akkadian names are known; one kind, for instance, seems likely to have been concerned with literary and musical forms of worship, and another with the flow not of sounds, but of celebratory inebriants and ablutions.

There would have been much music, with many instruments, with incantations and hymns at regular and precisely determined times accompanied by the odors of ceremonial substances, including the fat of sacrificed animals, burning.

The female version of the holy man was such mainly because she *was* female, just as Ishtar's femaleness, in Mesopotamian religion, was identified with her role as the goddess of sexuality; and it may have been the primary role of the priestesses of Ishtar to incarnate her in the annual re-enactment of the mythical marriage of the goddess with her lover, the shepherd Tammuz, whose role, it is thought, was taken by the king.

The representations of figures in the Marseille Tarot cards are very general, and the only really anomalous thing, in their obviously medieval context, is, of course, the idea of a high priestess at all; some commentators have gone so far as to suggest that it is a reference to a medieval legend about a woman who got herself elected pope by pretending to be a man, and was not found out until she actually gave birth in front of a crowd of people. Others have mentioned Joan of Arc. In view of the Mesopotamian origin and the equally obvious fact that they had priestesses then, there seems nothing to explain in that regard.

The High Priestess, as she is portrayed, enthroned and with an opened book, could, again, be based on any number of seated deities in the seal images; the one that appears here (Figure 49) seems as likely as any other and more likely than some, partly because of the close graphic correspondence and, partly, because it is Ea, a sort of priest himself in his compassion (if that is what it was) for mankind and his role as a wisdom-giver, and also because it is Ea again in the next one; and, perhaps most of all, because of the particular scene portrayed in this image.

It is the Judgment of Zu.

Who was Zu, and why were they judging him?

The Babylonian myth of the bird god Zu has thus far been recovered only in pieces, but it, like so many other Babylonian myths, is known to be an adaptation of an older Sumerian myth. Zu (also called Anzu; Sumerian Imdugud) lived in the under-world, and the deed around which the story appears to have been constructed was its theft of the Tablet of Destiny from the great god Enlil, which gave it Enlil's power – the greatest power, a complication that dissuaded the two gods Anu asked to kill Zu from attempting the task. Marduk, the Sumerian Lugulbanda, was not so timid, and succeeded in bringing Zu before Ea or Enlil – the seal shows Ea, but literary records more often refer to Enlil – to be judged.

Marduk, the son of Ea, had an earlier experience with this Tablet of Destiny when he took it from Kingu, the son of Tiamat, who, with Apsu, the other primordial god, gave birth to the great gods of the prevailing Sumerian pantheon, and slew Kingu and Tiamat for good measure.

The Tablet of Destiny or, to use the Sumerian word for it, the *me*, was a sort of divine template. They are sometimes referred to (whether by the ancients or by the translators) in the plural, the Tablets of Destiny. The *me* were, according to some, the property of Enki/Ea (even though Zu stole them from Enlil), and occupied a position of overwhelming importance in the religion of the

Sumerians and, hence, for the many people who took over their land and religion. They were the decrees of heaven, written before our world came into being, and formed the basis of all institutions and, even, every aspect of society, religion and civilization; from another point of view, they were discussed as including actual physical objects as well as abstractions, from musical instruments and artisanal tools to truth and lies, sex, various kinds of priest, victory and royal paraphernalia.

Let us consider this arrestingly un-primitive conception in light of the ideas discussed earlier about levels of reality emanating from a sublime source. Looking down, as it were, from God's point of view – and as blasphemous as that might sound, it is only an exercise to try to follow what the great teachers have said about how it really is – the First Intelligence was created; the Universal Soul was produced out of that; and the Intelligence then transmitted to the Soul – the Pen wrote on the Tablet – everything that was to be; and the World Soul made it, and continues to make it, happen. At some point, as Ibn al 'Arabi said in so many words, this means everything we know. As noted heretofore, in Sufi teaching as formulated classically within the Islamic context, God has attributes, which manifest as his names (*asma*), and these have some relationship with 'fixed entities' (*a'yan ath thabita*), in the sense that they are so in knowledge. There is, in fact, the *'alam al jabarut*, the 'world of (divine) power', beyond form; and there is the *'alam al mithal* or *'alam al khiyal*, the 'world of similitudes (or forms)' or 'world of imagination.' They are similitudes because they are not the 'real thing': they are the version of the real thing that we experience. In a sense, of course, the real thing is not a thing; which is to say, it is more 'real' than 'thing.'

It may be protested that it is Plato all over again. The problem there is that the idea of the Sumerian *me* was already ancient in Plato's time.

The question of whether there are such things as archetypes

that exist on some level, and on which everything that happens in what we call our world depends is, if true, obviously a serious one. It in turn raises questions concerning their nature, whether they change and, if so, how, and what the role, if any, is of human mentation in their activity.

Jung had his idea of archetypes, but it was characterized by his preoccupations as a psychiatrist, studying the individual and 'collective unconscious,' where potent images and patterns manifested themselves in the lives and dreams of the people who came to him seeking relief from their suffering. He has been criticized for overstepping the bounds of his discipline and entering the realm of religion, but what most people mean by religion in this context itself exemplifies an ignorance of the comprehensiveness of the knowledge of which we are seeking echoes.

So there are the divine ideas, or archetypes, or Tablet of Destiny. What else can be found out about them – or are they things only talked about in archaic formulations? The archaism of archaic formulation may be an obstacle only to the extent that we are unwilling to trouble ourselves both to overcome our own hidden assumptions of superiority, and forego the sense of drama that accompanies what we feel must be the tragedy of being modern and ignorant, and embrace the tedium of finding the lock, finding the key to the lock, and putting the key in the lock and turning it.

Is there a clue in the story of Noah's Ark?

Meanings of the word *nuh* ('nooh') in Arabic, as 'Noah' is rendered, include 'bewail the dead' (as he must have done) and 'turn to, set oneself to (do something)' (as he also did). From *nah* we get 'urge to haste, goad on' (and *nahih*, 'repeat a tone in the chest', reminiscent of the Sufi *dhikr*). *Niha* means 'end, limit, extent,' which the Flood certainly was. *Naih* is 'derive quiet from': in the original Mesopotamian version, the gods decided to destroy mankind because people were, simply, making too much noise. ('Noise' here, Gurdjieff would undoubtedly say, represents the dissonant emanations produced *en masse* by a less-than-top-quality species, the toxic energetic waste of a creature whose evolution had gone so badly astray as to impinge upon the very harmony of the spheres; and the 'sweet savor' of the smoke rising up to, and pleasing, God from the sacrificed animals that Noah offers after the waters have subsided and they are back on dry land, the restoration of those emanations to purity and excellence.) *Nauh*, with a different *h*, means 'be firm, courageous,' and 'fill without satiating' (as God did to the earth, with rain).

'Flood' is *tufan*, in the sense of 'deluge,' 'continuous rain' and, also, 'general mortality,' 'far-reaching storm or calamity' and 'great quantity.' *Tafanin* means 'lies, idle talk; holding back; remaining behind' (as most people did). *Tafnin*, differently spelled, is 'mixture' (recall Shah Waliullah and the mixed-together predications of the Divine Names, and also the idea that what seems to be evil is really a relationship between Names of conflicting meaning). The word from which *markab*, 'boat,' is derived is *rakaba*, 'travel on the sea.' As already seen, *raqaba* means 'watch, observe attentively'; and *baraka*, of course, is not only the word for what is traditionally thought of as the 'blessing' associated with Sufis that, among other things, protects and preserves, but also means 'rain continuously.'

As observed in the discussion of The Wheel of Fortune, 'animals' can be taken as representing the 'realities,' the 'divine ideas' or, if you like, archetypes. The word in Arabic, *haiwan*, means not only 'animal,' but 'anything living' and, even, 'life.' It is thus not difficult to see what is meant by one of each (gender) being on the boat, or Ark.

The world covered by water is, in effect, formless and uncreated: the 'blessed realities' are above it. It is the world 'above' and 'before' our own.

The nature of the connection between that world and ours, or at least something of the nature of the connection that can, in the current state of affairs, be made with it, is suggested by what

Noah does with the raven and the dove. The raven is robust and coarse compared with the delicate dove, somewhat like the relationship between left and right brain mentation, logic and intuition. Nothing can be learned about that realm by referring to the raven: the fact that it does not come back is no sure indication either that land has appeared, or that it hasn't, because it can just keep flying. The dove, representing a refinement of thinking, returns with an olive branch: Arabic for both 'olive' and 'olive oil' is *zait*: 'oil,' of course, is the same as 'essence,' and even sounds very much like *dhat*. The refinement to vanishing point, as it were, of the dove may represent a stage of mystical certainty; from our earthly point of view, perhaps, it can be seen as indicating a successful reception of some sort.

On the other hand, within the terms of the larger allegory, it may be that the detection of the presence of the olive tree – the source of the branch the dove brings back – represents something akin to the Kabbalistic *Ein Sof* that is both the origin of the *sefiroth* and the 'sap' that vivifies them: it indicates – or creates? – the 'dry land' where the 'animals,' the archetypes, can then manifest themselves.

In the text, the rainbow is supposed to be the sign of God's solemn 'promise' (*wa'd*, 'make a promise') that he will 'never' again destroy all living creatures; later, it specifically says, 'with a flood.' Associated meanings for *wa'd* include 'arrange' or 'appoint a time for,' 'threaten, menace' and, even, 'deadline.' Similar sounding words mean 'kill, destroy,' 'multiple, numerous,' and 'return' and 'recurrence.' (Remember also the *'Ad* people of the Koran.)

'The waters shall no more become a flood to destroy all flesh,' reads Chapter 9, verse 15 of Genesis. 'Water,' *ma'*, sounds almost exactly like *ma*, 'not,' indicating negation, of course; and the plural of 'water,' *miyah*, is like *mauh*, 'to mix' and, also, 'thin, dilute, adulterate; falsify, misrepresent'; and also like *maih*, 'to strut, swagger, walk with affected dignity.' The double negative carries a troubling implication, and there are evocations of deceit and the sort of behavior characteristic of the commanding self.

While the *Contemporary English Version* (largely drawn upon here) has God speaking of the rainbow as being 'in the sky,' the consensus of most other translations is that it should be as it appears in the *King James*: 'the bow shall be seen in the cloud,' and, 'the bow shall be in the cloud.' 'Bow' is *qus*; *ghash* means 'corruption, debasement, fraud, deceit,' and *kais*, 'intelligence, subtlety, gracefulness, elegance.' *Qiyas* is 'measurement, reference, scale, example, analogy, comparison.'

The primary word for 'clouds' in Arabic is *ghamam*, from *gham*, meaning 'cover, veil, conceal,' 'be obscure, incomprehensible' and, also, 'to fill with sadness, pain or grief.'

The notion of 'covering' overlaps with another range of words associated with *washy*, which means 'embellish, ornament with *many colors*, embroider (a fabric); slander, defame'; and 'fault, flaw, defect; mark, sign.' 'The rainbow will be the sign of that solemn promise,' reads Chapter 9, verse 17.

On one level, the message would appear to be that some disagreeable experiences, at least, contain something potentially valuable for those able to see through superficialities and appearances, perhaps by some kind of analogical approach.

Considered from yet another angle, and taking into account the possibility that the object portrayed in Figure 45 is, indeed, a rainbow, it may be that the rainbow and the animals, or their meaning, are meant to be considered in a closer relationship than is conveyed in the Noah's Ark story as we have it. The rainbow and the animals may simply be a symbolic representation of that cyclic manifestation of Divine Names mentioned in the context of our discussion of The Wheel of Fortune. Ishtar, in that case, would represent the World Soul, from which they all leave and to which they all return.

Returning to Zu, however, it almost seems that the message is that accidents can happen even on the level of reality to which the

Tablet of Destiny pertains. What could this possibly mean?

Readers of Gurdjieff's major work, *Beelzebub's Tales to His Grandson* (Beelzebub's grandson is Hussein, which, of course, was the name of one of the grandsons of the Prophet Mohammed), will be familiar with his story of how, in extremely distant times, long before anything like what is meant by 'history,' the earth was struck by a comet that resulted in the formation of the moon, which in turn had all sorts of untoward consequences for the kind of life the human race was obliged, in time, to lead. This account of the origin of the moon, again, has now attained the status of accepted fact in the mainstream scientific community. Anomalous artifacts that have been discovered (and that the mainstream scientific community has set itself to ignoring as firmly as Noah set himself to making his Ark) – for example, what appear to be shoeprints in earth known to be hundreds of millions of years old – make one wonder whether the rest of this story is not somehow literally true as well. The idea is that man's evolution was stunted or in some other way went wrong as a result of and, perhaps, as a temporarily unavoidable adaptation to, a cataclysm. In particular, says Gurdjieff, the new satellite of this planet necessitated modifications to the human race, and the only way to ensure that humans would be reconciled to their new predicament was by blunting their perception of reality: and the way to do this was to induce congenital egotism, which may be what is meant by the terms in which Marduk is depicted. Where the correct and harmonious manifestation of the archetypes or Divine Ideas in our realm is concerned, such a development would be susceptible to being recorded allegorically in a story like the myth of Zu, where Zu – an entity of horrifying destructive power from the sky – representing the comet, 'stole' the 'Tablet of Destiny': in other words, interrupted the ordered expression, in our world, of the Divine Ideas.

Translated cuneiform accounts of the Zu drama refer to Enlil having 'made an extra destiny' for the bird god, and emphasize that in stealing the Tablet of Destiny, Zu stole kingship itself from Enlil, one major consequence of which was that the rites of religion ceased to be performed. Appeals to various heroes to go to Zu's mountain hideaway and get the Tablet back are appeals to their vanity, telling how celebrated they will be. As the hero who does take up the challenge – Marduk in some accounts, others, such as Ninurta, in others – sets out, he is encouraged to obscure Zu's perception of him with a fog; then, when he attacks with bow and arrow, Zu, using the power bestowed on him by his possession of the Tablet, orders the various constituents of the bow and arrow, such as the feathers and the reed of the arrow and the string made of the innards of a ram, to return to their original natural conditions, which they do, possibly representing a stage before the action of the *me*, the Divine Ideas; and humanity can only cope with it by not seeing things too clearly.

Figure 53. Detail (reversed) of cylinder seal, 990-660 BCE, showing a priest of the god Adad dancing ecstatically. British Museum.

Figure 51 shows Ea in his house in the water, with other figures, including Shamash, around. It is interesting to see how the kneeling person on the right, who is grasping or supporting some sort of pole (we considered him in relation to the Strength card), and the god on the left with one knee raised for the climb have become the supplicants who have their backs turned to us in the High Priest card. It even appears that the vortexes in the lower corners, left and right, in the water-stream at the bottom of Ea's dwelling have become the backs of the supplicants' heads.

The opinion of historians is that the individual shown in Figure 53 – the original is right side up – is the priest spoken of in the seal's accompanying inscription. Adad, again, is another name for Enlil and is, supposedly, represented by the winged disk to which the priest is raising his arms. His mid-air position may indicate that he is performing some act of ritual worship, or that he is dancing ecstatically, as did the dervishes of the god Baal on Mount Carmel who are mentioned in the eighteenth chapter of the first book of Kings in the Hebrew Bible.

**Figure 54. Tarot.
The Hanged Man.**

The reason for showing him upside-down here should be obvious. Someone else, a few hundred years ago, also saw him that way.

The origin of the name, 'The Hanged Man,' may be not that hard to discern: the inclusion of the word 'man' could be what gives it away. The importance has been marked of the Sufi teaching concerning what they call *al insan al kamil*, the 'perfect' or 'complete man.' *Insan* is 'man', *kamil* is 'complete'. Another word for 'entire, total, universal' is *kulliya(t)*. Arabic for 'hanged' is *'alaq*. Someone may very well have misread or misheard *insan al kulliya(t)* as *insan al 'alaq*.

That leaves the question: what gave them the idea of a 'hanged man' in the first place?

There is a story so old that in some renditions it takes place in Babylon, although versions or traces of it are found in ancient Sanskrit, in Zoroastrian and Armenian literature, in the Talmud and in the Koran and, also, in Rumi's *Mathnawi*. It is the story of Harut and Marut.

What follows here is the version of Muhammad bin Khavendshah bin Mahmud, 'commonly called Mirkhond,' the fifteenth century CE Bokharan author of a standard Persian language history of ancient prophets and other important people entitled *Rauzat as-Safa*, or 'Garden of Purity,' as translated by

Edward Rehatsek, and published by the Royal Asiatic Society in 1881.

'Some historians have said that when Edris attained felicity, according to the verse, 'And we raised him to an exalted station,' he became in the upper world an associate of angels, who mistook him for Adam, saying: 'What seeketh the sinner among an assembly which never transgressed?' The Absolute Sage (i.e. God) did not approve of these words, and reproached them as follows: 'Had you been in the position of men you would have likewise sinned; and in order to cause this truth to become evident to all, I command you to select some of yourselves, whom I shall appoint to execute a certain business.' Then the inhabitants of the upper world chose the three following individuals: A'za, A'zaya, and A'zayil. The Lord commanded them to descend upon the earth, and to rule the inhabitants thereof with rectitude; to participate with them in eating, drinking and in their appetites; to worship Him, but to kill no one unjustly, neither to drink wine, nor to commit adultery. The three angels agreed to all this. They arrived on earth, associated with mankind, occupied themselves by day in governing, and returned at night to heaven, stripping off their humanity when ascending, and re-assuming it when descending.

'One of the three intended to rebel, was therefore excused from reigning, and was at his own request again allowed to enter the ranks of the saints in heaven. The two remaining ones, who were surnamed Harut and Marut, remained on the throne of dominion and continued to rule.

'Meanwhile, a handsome female, unsurpassed in amenity and beauty, who was in Arabic called Zohra, in Syriac Nahid, in Persian Beedukht, came one day on business to these two angels. When they beheld Zohra's beauty they were inclined towards her, kept their desires concealed from each other, but ascertained her dwelling-place, and told her to return to it, and that after duly investigating her affair they would get it settled. She accordingly went to her house, and both the angels hastened to the same place, unknown to each other, anxiously endeavouring to meet her. They, however, happened to meet each other at her door, and were thus forced to reveal their mutual aspirations. They asked Zohra for permission to enter, after obtaining which they began to declare to her their love.

'She replied: 'Your religion is different from mine; I shall not obey you until you worship my idol.' The angels replied: 'This culpable deed will never be committed by us, since the Most High never pardons the sin of associating (with Him) another in His worship.'

'Zohra continued: 'If you will not adore my idol, then teach me the ineffable name by the power of which you ascend to heaven.' They again refused, whereon Zohra said: 'I have a pretty maidservant; I shall give her to you instead of myself.' They said: 'We want thee! How could a person elect a substitute for one who has no equal?' Zohra continued: 'Some pure wine is at hand; if you drink some of that I shall comply with your wishes.'

'Harut and Marut agreed that this was the easiest thing of all she asked them to do. When they had partaken of the wine, and become intoxicated, they worshipped the idol and told Zohra the ineffable name.

'At that time a man arrived among them and became aware of all that had happened. Zohra told them that this man knew their evil deeds, and that it would be best to kill him, lest he should put them to shame among the people. Harut and Marut arose, and in their drunkenness separated the head of that luckless individual from his body.

'Zohra then ascended to heaven by the power of the ineffable name she had learnt from them.

'After the base acts which Harut and Marut had committed, the Absolute Sovereign spoke thus to the angels: 'Have you seen the state of those elected by yourselves?' The angels replied: 'O

Lord! Thou knowest thy servants best.'

'When Harut and Marut awoke from the sleep of their drunk-enness they became convinced of their perdition, and began to weep. At that time Jebrail, the faithful spirit, arrived from the Powerful Avenger, and taking part in their lamentations said: 'The Almighty – whose name be praised – has given you the choice between the punishment in this or in the next world.' They replied: 'The misery of this world is transient, and will cease, but condemnation in the next will last for ever; therefore we select punishment in this world.'

'Accordingly they were *suspended upside down* in the well of Babel, where they must remain till the day of resurrection. Their most acute torment consists in their becoming from time to time prey to carnal lusts to a degree which it is impossible to conceive. It has been related that Jebrail has taught them a word which, if pronounced at a time lust is at its highest, will appease it.

'In some histories it is narrated that a man, having acquired great proficiency in magic, died. His son was exceedingly anxious to learn this science, but was told by an old sorcerer to whom he had been directed that he could never do so unless he paid a visit to Harut and Marut. The said sorcerer conducted the youth to a cave situated between two mountains, and told him not to mention the name of Allah in the presence of these two. He agreed, whereon the old sorcerer beckoned to him to enter. After proceeding a considerable distance in the cavern, the young man heard the roaring of a dreadful voice, and beheld two men suspended upside down from a gibbet; but when he saw their eyes shining like torches he lost his self-possession, and exclaimed: 'No god but Allah, and Muhammad is His prophet!' The two angels trembled at these words, saying, 'O young man! It is a long time since we have heard these words. Do the inhabi-tants of the earth at present utter them?' The youth replied, 'Yes.' They inquired for the reason for his coming, after hearing which they dissuaded him from learning sorcery, and said to him: 'Our joy is near, for the resurrection is at hand.' The youth accepted their advice, and returned from that place repentant and sad. The strangeness of this narrative has caused its extension to this length.'[19] [Emphasis mine.]

The Koran itself – which Muslims, of course, believe to be the words of God as delivered to Mohammed by the Archangel Gabriel (the 'faithful spirit' Jebrail of the above account) – is, as always, riveting on the subject:

'And when there came to them an Apostle from God, confirming what was with them, a party of the People of the Book threw away the Book of God behind their backs, as if it had been something they did not know! They followed what the evil ones gave out falsely against the power of Solomon; the blasphemers were, not Solomon, but the evil ones, teaching men magic, and such things as came down at Babylon to the angels Harut and Marut. But neither of these taught anyone such things without saying: 'We are only for trial; so do not blaspheme.' They learned from them the means to sow discord between man and wife. But they could not thus harm anyone except by God's permission. And they learned what harmed them, not what profited them.' (Sura 2, verses 101 and 102.)

One spelling of Zohra's name, zahar, means 'shine, sparkle, be brilliant; the best or most exquisite part of a thing'; and also, 'the planet Venus.' Another, zahr, means 'forget, neglect; wealth, power, strength; anything neglected, absent, hidden; intelligence, information.' A similar spelling to zahr is zahir, meaning 'external, exoteric, superficial, exterior, surface' (and which is often contrasted with batin, 'interior' or 'esoteric': these terms are applied to interpretation of the Koran, for instance). Similar in sound is sahr, 'magic, sorcery; anything captivating, charming, fascinating, deceiving, deluding.' As mentioned earlier, shahr is a word for 'moon' and, also, for 'publish, make known,' and for 'draw and brandish the sword,' as Shamash brandishes his saw on rising.

The specific nature of the 'trouble' supposed to be caused by the magic learned from Harut and Marut is 'between a man and his wife.' A word for 'marriage' is *sur*. It is the angels' desire to engage in 'coition,' *sar*, with Zohra that leads them astray and causes them to divulge their 'secret' – *sirr* – and thus lose their 'power of authority,' *saur(at)* and 'rank, degree, dignity,' *suwar*.

Babel (the Koranic verse refers to 'Babeela') was, and is, famous for its 'tower'; the angels are suspended in a 'well': external and internal, apparent and hidden, *zahir* and *batin* (or *sirr*). The Babelites who built the tower were dispersed through 'confusion of tongues,' the infliction of manifold misunderstandings: in this story, 'secrets' are constantly being revealed, and everyone sooner or later understands each other all too well.

It is a commonplace of Sufi literature that mankind's perception of reality is upside-down, and that the Sufi, who is really right-side-up, seems upside-down to 'normal' people. Harut and Marut thought they were better than humans (which was also Iblis' mistake); the desire for power and ascendancy leads to their opposites. The angels' experiences on earth might also be seen as alluding to the experiences of a Sufi aspirant, with themes of service, 'passionate love,' 'intoxication,' patience, and so on, but especially to the phenomenon of losing one's flattering illusions about oneself that is said to be necessary before learning can take place, and to be one of the first things that may happen after the would-be student is engaged by a teaching source. Even the theme of beheading ('head' is *ras*) is supposed to represent an act or condition of surrendering, placing oneself in the hands of a spiritual guide. From this point of view, 'magic,' *sahr*, may be just a code word for the path of devotion to *zahar*, Venus, 'love.' The 'discord' that students or would-be students of 'magic' seek to produce may, then, represent the 'discord' of rescuing a sublime reality from earthly stagnation and stasis. It is noteworthy that the third angel, who went down with Harut and Marut, wanted to rebel – presumably a grievous sin; yet he was not only not punished, but allowed to return to heaven: unless, in the context of this 'upside-down' interpretation, that *is* a punishment. Within another context, he could be a student who had fewer grandiose ideas about his own worth and, thus, had less need of experiences to dissolve them.

Zohra, Venus, is Ishtar. In the myth of her descent into the underworld, she escapes by arranging to have Tammuz substitute for her, which it turns out may be a way of saying that when people get through with distorting a teaching about higher reality, all they are left with is their own tendency to turn something alive and uncontrollable into something as docile as a sheep. One way of reading the Harut and Marut story may be to see their 'substituting' for her as having the same significance. One of the meanings of *nabi* is 'deputy,' who is a substitute for the higher authority. People come to the Tarot cards wanting to learn a kind of magic...

None of this is to discount the importance of the fact that, for instance, there is a basic practical – if you like, psychological – relationship between secrets and power. Arabic for 'hair' is *sha'r*. In fact, if meanings of words that sound like *sirr* and *sar* and *sha'r* are considered altogether, one of the things they can be assembled into is the story of Samson in the Biblical Book of Judges.

'Once so strong and mighty,' the *Contemporary English Version* has him saying, in the 'riddle' he composed after he found the lion he had slain earlier with his bare hands had bees living in the carcass, and he had sampled their honey, ' — now so sweet and tasty!'

'When the seeker of truth,' Attar records Abu al Hasan Khirqani as saying, 'has cheerfully tasted poison nine times, on the tenth time he tastes sugar...To me it is as if there is something I do not know but that is in my stomach and that feeds me. It is as sweet as honey and as fragrant as musk. The world does not know in what way I am fed.'

Figure 55. Detail of Assyrian cylinder seal, 900 BCE, showing priests of the Canaanite goddess Athirat or Ashera. British Museum.

Athirat and Ashera are thought to be Canaanite versions of Ishtar.

Who is The Hermit?

Is he a seeker? Or a finder?

The notion of a hermit as someone occupied with austerities and self discipline has obvious connections with the idea of self restraint, such as may be intended in Temperance and, perhaps, Strength, and possibly with restraint and imprisonment imposed from without, as may be portrayed in The Hanged Man.

This hermit, though, seems to be on the move. He holds up a lamp, which – unless he is supposed to be Diogenes, who went around with a lamp in the daytime and, when asked why, said he was looking for an honest man – obviously indicates that he is in the dark. He has a walking stick, which he is holding in front of him in a way that he would if he were using it.

After Gilgamesh has seen his best friend die, and decided he had better think about that; and has set out to find Utnapishtim;

Figure 56. Tarot. The Hermit.

and has reached the mountains at the edge of the world; and has heard all that the scorpion men have had to say to try and talk him out of it; and has decided to carry on anyway, he proceeds past them, and embarks on a long journey through total, unrelenting darkness on his way to the sea.

In view of the fact that the individual shown in the card is, apparently, intended to be old, it is more likely that he is meant to be someone who has found than someone who is still seeking. He appears to be heavily cloaked, which is consistent with his hermetic or hidden status. Perhaps he is the High Priest on an errand.

Perhaps he, as one who has found, is out and around in order to meet the Fool, who is still seeking. Ghazali quotes Mohammed, quoting God: 'When he (the seeker) comes to me on foot, I go to him quickly.' Likewise, Ibn Abbas said, 'When I sought knowledge I was humbled; but when knowledge sought me, I was exalted'.

Figure 57. Detail of Uruk period (3500 to 3000 BCE) cylinder seal showing a priest with a ceremonial gift. Directorate General of Antiquities, Baghdad.

Bearing in mind that Mohammed claimed not to bring a new religion, but to restore the original one of Ibrahim – Abraham – elsewhere in the *Ihya*, Ghazali quotes a presumably long since lost Abrahamic scripture in which, as in the Koran, God speaks in the first person:

'Good men seek Me with alacrity; they have truth in their hearts and are on the correct path. They are happy because they will be rewarded for what they have earned with their right hands. When they come to Me out of their graves, light will go forward ahead of them, and they will be surrounded by angels.'

It is, thus, not inconceivable that the scene portrayed in the Hermit card originally was drawn from a source that was also the source of the name for the card Judgment.

Kabbalistic authors speak of 'the Ancient One,' 'the Ancient of the Ancient Ones,' and 'the Ancient of Days.' It is sometimes meant as a reference to the first *sefirah*, *Kether*, 'Crown.'

Figure 58. Tarot. Page of Clubs.

In the (probably medieval in time of composition) *Zohar*, 'Rabbi Schimeon' is quoted as saying, 'Only through secrecy is the world secure; and if secrecy is so important in worldly affairs, how much more is it necessary in matters of the most secret of secrets, and in the reflections of the Ancient of Days: matters that are not revealed, even, to the highest angels.'

The same dimension may be enlarged upon by noting that the Arabic word for 'old,' *qadam*, also means 'step,' in the literal sense and in all its metaphorical implications of 'stage,' 'precedence,' and 'going before.' The term 'Ancient One' is used by Sufis both to mean the sheikh, or teacher, and God; and, in this respect, it obviously resembles the *haqiqa al muhammad*, the 'Reality of Mohammed,' a continuum comprising the living teacher, Mohammed the Prophet himself, the archetype of the teacher or guide and, by extension, the source of all archetypes or 'divine ideas.'

In the context of the card image and the words of Rabbi Schimeon, there are even further reverberations of meaning detectable.

In writing of the Bektashi Order of dervishes, a nineteenth century European scholar observed that their mealtime grace finished with the words, 'by the Breath of the 3, the 5, the 7, and the 40 True Saints, – we thank Thee!'

He went on to explain:

'These numbers refer to the *rijal-ghaib* (or the unseen men), who every morning are supposed to attend at the Ka'aba (Caaba) of Makka, and who wander over the whole world, by Divine Command, to superintend the affairs of mankind. Of the first three, one is called the *qutb*, or centre, – the second and third the *umana*, or the Faithful. One stands on the right and the other on the left of the *qutb*, and they all stand on the summit of the Ka'aba. They are also called the *ahl-i-tasarruf* (Owners or Masters of Destiny), and they never leave Makka. There are also four others, called *autad* (the Great or Eminent), who wander over the world. The seven are called the *akhiar*, or the 'Very good,' who equally wander over the surface of the globe. The 40 are called the *shuhada*, or the victims, and their mission is equally the same. There are also 70 others, called the *budala* (plural of *abdal*), or the servants of Allah; also eight, called the *nuqba*, or the deputies, and their duties are much like those of the others.

'All of these go to Makka every morning, and report the result of their previous day's peregrinations to the *qutb* or centre, offer up prayers, and set out anew.'[20] (In fact, *qutb* means 'pole' or 'axis,' not 'center'; *tasarruf* means 'control' or 'influence'; *autad* means 'the firm ones,' not 'the Great or Eminent'; and *abdal* means 'changed' or 'substitute,' not 'servant.')

A further particularization of this idea, that there are individuals of a high spiritual station who, unknown to the mass of humanity, perform functions vital to the continued existence of our planet and the life it supports, including humanity, is in the character of Khidr, 'The Green One,' spoken of by Sufis as a (usually) hidden guide who: may be a prophet; may be Elijah, who has never died; is a teacher and initiator into wisdom; and who uses his supernatural powers to affect events in the world in a way that may be incomprehensible to those who cannot see what he sees.

No less a Sufi than Ibn al 'Arabi claimed that Khidr was his initiator. In his massive work *Openings in Mecca*, he wrote:

'There was another time when I was aboard a boat in Tunis' port. My stomach troubled me but, as the others were asleep, I went and looked at the sea. The moon was full, and by its light I suddenly saw a figure approaching on the water's surface. Eventually he came and stood nearby; he raised, first, one leg, so that I could see that it was dry, and then the other. We talked for a while, and then he made his salutations and left, heading for a lighthouse on a hill more than two miles away. In reaching it, he took only two or three steps, and I heard his orisons from there. He was a frequent visitor to al Kinani, a sheikh of our order, at whose house I had been that night. Later, when I was again in the town, I met a man who asked me about my night aboard the boat, and about meeting Khidr, and what we had discussed.

Elsewhere he relates how he went to visit a certain Ali ibn Abdallah bin Jami, a man devoted to austerities:

'He directed me to sit in a certain place and, when I asked why, he explained that Khidr had just been sitting there, and he told me to take that spot for the blessing that imbued it.'

The host went on to say that Khidr had produced a small cotton cap, and put it on the host's head; the host then took it off, kissed it, and put it between Khidr and himself. Then Khidr asked Ali if he wanted him to invest him with the *khirqa* (cloth mantle that represents initiation into the Sufi *tariqa*); the initiation by Khidr himself is, the host told Ibn al 'Arabi, the highest form. On the occasion in question, Khidr invested the host, Ali, and Ali in turn invested Ibn al 'Arabi; in the course of his life, the latter received the initiation of Khidr a total of three times.

In Arabic, a hermit is a *zahid*, with an emphasis on austerity of life in the cause of religion. The Arabic letter *dal*, at the end of *zahid*, is not very different in appearance on the page from *ra*, as in 'Zohra.' It is entirely conceivable that it was simply misread by the artist or artists who put together the Tarot cards. Another possibility is its similarity in sound to *sahid*, which means 'be sleepless, vigilant,' which is one way of looking at a different card (The Chariot).

Shown because of their striking conformity are another seal picture of yet another priest, an even older one, from Sumer, in a similar attitude, and the only Minor Arcana Tarot card we will be looking at, the Page of Clubs.

One more potential Hermit-source goes in a

Figure 59. Detail, showing Usmu, the attendant of Ea, from cylinder seal showing Shamash rising.

different direction.

The individual in Figure 59 has been said to be Usmu, the attendant of Ea, with his two faces. It is possible that he, too, contributed to the Hermit card, which would not be inconsistent with his role as the representative of the God of Wisdom.

Refer again to Figure 47. Pan left: all the way left.

Whatever may be said of this Fool (Figure 62), he cannot be accused of rushing in.

The lion (either it is a little one, or the fellow is very big; if it is a god, he is) and the bow and arrow clearly suggest warlike preoccupations: which, in turn, suggest – since it is male, and Ishtar is accounted for – that the god shown is either Enlil or Nergal. He could also be a hunter, like the one in Figure 61.

The Fool became the Joker, and the Joker, like war, is wild.

The Fool is the Ignorant One, who may or may not know he is a fool and, to that extent, is or is not un-foolish, and is a seeker of the knowledge that will make him even less of a fool. On the path he is either on or has a chance of finding – since one thing you can say for sure about him is that he is walking and, therefore, covering ground – he may meet The Hermit, if he is lucky. It is an odd

Figure 60. Detail, showing unknown god, from same seal as Figure 59.

Figure 61. Detail of Akkad period cylinder seal showing an unidentified god holding a club and other objects, and with leaping sheep. British Museum.

**Figure 62. Tarot.
The Fool.**

beast hanging on to him: is he in pain? Does he even know it's there? Is he oblivious and, by implication, insensitive and stupid, by nature, or is his discipline so great as to make it *look* the same, but with all the interior difference in the world?

Is what appears to be an animal part of his own nature, rendered visibly to signify his developed, painful consciousness of it, and a remedy for which is the whole cause of his seeking? Or is the fact that he is looking forward, up, and away from it an indication that it is precisely what he is not yet aware of, but must become aware of if he is to be anything other than a fool?

Gurdjieff said that the organ affixed to man to blunt his perceptions and dull the pain of awareness of his predicament after the primeval disaster was attached to the base of man's spine.

An Arabic word for 'stupid, idiotic' is *balid* ('baleed'). Another word, the preposition *ba*, means 'with, by, at, in, to, towards': *balid*, 'fool,' could thus be, for instance, *ba al add*, '(man) with strength' or 'victory,' as was Gilgamesh.

There is another word, however, even more interesting, which means not only 'stupid, foolish, mad,' but also 'wanderers, travelers.' It is transliterated *'atahiyyat*. The first letter in this word is the glottal *'ain*. There are two letters in the Arabic alphabet that are both represented in English by 't' and, also, two letters shown by an 'h.' Change the *'ain* in *'atahiyyat* to the first letter of the Arabic alphabet, *alef*; change the one *t* letter to the other; change the *h* to the other *h*; and remove the long *ya* that gives you the 'ee' sound in -*hiyy*-. What does that produce?

A word that sounds similar, but has another meaning altogether: *itahat*.

It means, 'decree of fate.'

As in, 'destiny.'

As in, 'Tablet of Destiny.'

In fact, if you look again, closely, at Figure 49, which shows the Judgment of Zu – whose transgression, again, was that he stole the Tablet of Destiny, and took off with it until Marduk got it back, after which Zu was delivered to Ea – it is not difficult to see how either the figure of Zu himself in the middle, with some restraining device across the back of his neck and his bird-tail projecting out behind him, much where the Fool's too-friendly pet is, or the god on the extreme left with a plough over his shoulder, or both of them, have contributed significantly to the figure on The Fool card.

The Fool's historical remaking as the Joker of the modern playing card deck suggests an aspect that is, in a sense, other than the one already considered but, in another sense, is a deepening of it: the wise man pretending to be a fool as part of his wisdom.

Examples in literature are profuse of Sufis issuing what seems to be an invitation to interpret their behavior as a wish to get rid of somebody when it is, possibly, rather a matter of upsetting expectations and, especially, reflecting the would-be student's own mind to him. (If they really want to put someone off, one would think that accomplishment of the objective could well include preservation of the subject's ignorance.)

Shibli must have seemed like one kind of fool when he, an intelligent and capable man, followed the instructions of Junayd and sold sulfur, begged, and went from door to door looking for people he might have offended during his career as a civil servant in order to apologize to them. He must have seemed like another kind of fool when he first put sugar in the mouths of those who repeated the name of God; and then, as his 'state' increased, offered gold to those who would repeat it for him; and finally, when anyone repeated it, came after them with a sword because, he said, he had realized that they were only doing so out of mechanical habit.

It was of the other kind of fool – the one convinced that a fool is the last thing he would be – that Mohammed said that his foolishness was more harmful than the wickedness of the evil doer, in one of the better known traditions. Ghazali, for his part, does not hesitate to call fools those who, for instance, take literally anthropomorphic references to God, and observes that, as far as those 'unlearned' are concerned, the adherents of gnosis seem to them, likewise, fools.

Figure 63. Ea.

**Figure 64. Tarot.
The Chariot.**

Ea, as seen before, in his house under the water, is here (Figure 63) again:there is something of him and of this seal image in The Chariot (Figure 64). The god on the left and the unidentified crouching person on the right, who became the supplicants in The High Priest, have here undergone the indignity of transformation into horses, while Ea's dwelling itself has become the chariot.

Figure 65, though, which has also contributed, presents something new in that it would seem to indicate a specific relationship between two major deities in such a manner that, whether or not it illustrates a scene in a myth, it shows an interdependence that, in turn, implies limitations on their respective parts: which, of course, is not something one immediately associates with deities; you expect them to be able to pretty much do whatever they want. In this may

Figure 65. Ishtar standing on a lion yoked to the chariot of Enlil or Adad. Pierpont Morgan Library, New York.

be no more than the working-out of the relationship of lesser powers with the greater one, if one is inclined to think of it that way.

Assuming that it is given to us like this because there is something in it that is important for us to understand, it also implies a certain ordering and a discipline to achieve an end: clear links, again, with Strength, Temperance, and so on.

Enlil, if it is his chariot, is one of the highest gods, older, more powerful and more 'important' than Ishtar. It was from him – in most accounts, anyway – that the Tablet of Destiny was stolen by Zu, and he who judged Zu on its return by Marduk. It was he who tried to destroy mankind with the Flood that Utnapishtim escaped with Ea's help. Obviously he has something of a temper, and perhaps it is this aspect that is significant in the context of his being yoked to the goddess of love.

On another level, the chariot itself has been, as seen when discussing the Kabbalah, a metaphor for a metaphysical reality, regardless of whether it is accurate to see it and the usage just given as forming a continuum. The association of its status in that regard with what became the doctrine of the *sefiroth* in Jewish teaching is controversial: but then, as has also been shown, the *sefiroth* as they became and as they started out are different. The earliest Jewish sources using the term do so in the context of describing the ecstatic travels of the mystic through seven stages, formulated as temples or palaces, on his way to the throne of God. During the course of that journey, he becomes privy to all sorts of revelations about angels and magical procedures that culminate in the vision of the Creator, including gnosis of the structure of the Creator's own person, like the vision Ezekiel had, wherein he beheld God in a form resembling the primordial human and, also, as the lover in the Biblical Song of Solomon.

As far as the dervishes are concerned, *muraqaba* is the name they give to the contemplative and prayerful state, associated with wakefulness and the prevailing of the powers of the soul over the body while the two are yet united. They have a different name, *insila*, for the condition where the soul takes leave of the physical frame and wanders unfettered by space or time. It is sometimes asserted that the Prophet Mohammed was in such a state when he went on his night time journey, carried by the angelic horse *Buraq*.

These themes, of concentration, absorption, motivation and motion, a higher energy and, even, of untutoredness and Foolish oblivion are, perhaps, fittingly combined in another of Ibn al 'Arabi's accounts, where he is talking about a Sufi sheikh named al Kumi:

'Before I had read Qushayri's *Letter* or the work of any other teacher and, in fact, before I even realized that any of our path had committed anything to writing, and I was still ignorant of the vocabulary of the Sufis, I encountered the Sheikh al Kumi on an occasion I should relate. Having got on his horse, he indicated that another of our company and I should go and see him on a certain mountain a few miles from Seville. The next morning, after they had opened the gate of the city, my friend, with his copy of Qushayri, and I went and ascended the mountain, where we found our teacher with a servant who was looking after his horse. After prayers in the mosque that was on the mountain, the sheikh turned and, with his back to the niche indicating the direction of Mecca, put the copy of Qushayri's *Letter* in my hands, and ordered me to read aloud. I was so much in awe of him that I was incoherent, and dropped the book, so he instructed the other fellow to do the reading and, as he did so, the sheikh discoursed on the text. Thus we continued until late afternoon and it was time for prayers again.

'Our teacher then suggested that we should go back to the city and, mounting his horse, he started off, with me running beside him and hanging on to the stirrup. In the mean time he spoke about Abu Madyan, his qualities and his miracles. So completely entranced was I, with my attention the whole time on him up on his horse, that I didn't notice anything else.

'Abruptly, he turned and looked at me, and smiled; and dug his spurs into the horse, so that I had to run faster to stay with him.

'Then, stopping, he said: 'Look, and see what is behind you.'

'I looked and, as far as I could see, the path had thorn bushes up to my waist, and thorns completely covered the ground.

''Look at your feet and clothes,' he said.

'I did, and nowhere on them was there any evidence of the thorns.

''Such are the results of the blessing generated by our having talked of Abu Madyan. Persevere on our path, and you will certainly be saved.''

'Spurring his horse, he left. I learned a great deal from him.'

'The multiform body of the world lies open,' wrote the reclusive Hermeticist Mary Anne Atwood in England in the nineteenth century, 'but the source is everywhere occult.'[21] Hundreds of years earlier, in his apartments over Al Aqsa Mosque in Jerusalem, Ghazali observed, 'God has written on all things in a writing without words.'

Whoever can read that writing, of course, does not need to learn to 'read' the Tarot, because he can already 'read' anything. For the rest of us, perhaps, the Tarot may be considered a kind of exercise in the same general direction.

Does everything we have examined mean that there are no other legitimate interpretations of the Tarot?

Why should it? Even proceeding on the assumption – and, as we have seen, there is good evidence for it – that the Sufis are in some way responsible for the Tarot, it is also clear that it is not too much of an exaggeration to say that there is more than one Tarot. How do we know that there was not some even earlier and now, in itself, completely unknown body of material onto which everything we have been considering was grafted? Moreover, Sufis maintain that the scriptures of all true religions, including the Koran, are susceptible to multiple levels of interpretation. Why should the Tarot be any different?

There is even an historical example of someone whose Sufi credentials have been endorsed and who wrote what is manifestly an interpretation of the Tarot in frankly esoteric terms that also, however, appear somewhat idiosyncratic.

An English diplomat and knight named Fairfax Cartwright in 1899 published a book entitled *The Mystic Rose From the Garden of the King: A Fragment of The Vision of Sheikh Haji Ibrahim of Kerbala.* Notwithstanding the attribution, it was his own work. It has been republished more than once.

The Tarot references are explicit.

A 'Mystic Dervish' is interrogated by a 'King' about experiences he has found particularly educative. The dervish tells of coming across a 'Temple built like a Tower' to the interior of which he is admitted by a 'venerable old man,' the 'Sage of the Temple.' The sage asks him about his 'strength and determination' for the quest for knowledge and ability to 'climb to the topmost chamber.' The dervish asks the sage to be his guide, and he conducts him into what he calls the 'Temple of Human

Knowledge.' Once within, the dervish realizes that the tower itself is triangular, with a circular colonnade (row of columns supporting a roof), and that the wall behind the colonnade is 'covered with representations of human figures, and my Guide spoke: 'Behold, the Cycle of Human Life! See Man as he appeareth to the human eye!"

The first picture the seeker sees is of 'the Childhood of Man,' and the description of the children sounds very much like the mood evoked by the Sun card; the 'Angel of Life was drawing back the Veil,' though, 'beyond which lay the World with all its dangers and possibilities.' 'Satan' lurks in 'the darkness by the Veil,' beyond which is the 'Promised Land' toward which 'the children full of joyance were marching,' and the Angel looks at them with 'pity' as Satan marks 'with his claws upon the sand the number of those whom he would devour.' We have The Sun, Judgment, The World, The Devil; and that is only the beginning. In this case Judgment is, indeed, a beginning and not an end, it seems.

Each child, the seeker realizes, 'represented some type of Humanity.' It sounds as if he is watching something like the entry of souls into the material world: in other words, incarnation. 'One maiden I noticed gazing earnestly at the Star of Love, which from above shone down upon the World of Youth, and another maiden – in whom was the soul of the wanton – was bending down to the ground to pluck a rose, and in her haste to seize it a thorn had pricked her finger.' Here is The Star, only bending not to pour but to pluck.

The guide leads him into the tower and explains the design of it, how it 'containeth seven levels, and on each level are three Chambers, and above all lieth one Chamber, and the ascent thereto is long and wearisome.' With the guide going before him the seeker starts up, having visions of a fairly obviously allegorical significance in each chamber. Some of the figures and other elements in the visions are easily identifiable with particular Tarot cards; others are more difficult. The first, for instance, is an arresting description of being plunged into darkness, prompting the seeker to pray, 'craving in humility of spirit for illumination,' after which he finds his head illuminated while his feet 'remained lost in the darkness of unreality.' What follows sounds like an allusion to The Hanged Man, but with a novel interpretation:

'I knew that the Soul of Man – the reflection of the Unity – is suspended between the Light and the Darkness, and through the opposition of the Light and the Darkness the Soul of Man gains consciousness of the Unknown which veils the Eternal Unity. And the mystic symbol of the Unity shone forth upon the walls of this Chamber.' There follow visions of a veiled female with a book, who tells him, 'I am the Recipient – the Passive; I am the complement of that which thou hast seen in the First Chamber. I am the link between the Unity and Man'; another throned woman, 'wearing the Crown of Authority,' who tells him, 'I am the Law of the World; with my Sceptre do I govern it'; and further, individuals who would appear to be modeled on the High Priest, the Knight of the Minor Arcana, Justice, and so on. Some of them, as we have already indicated, seem to interpret one Tarot card in a variety of ways.

The visions of the seeker in *The Mystic Rose From the Garden of the King* culminate in a chamber into which his guide tells him he must enter alone. He finds himself once again engulfed in darkness; and again he prays, 'seeking for Illumination, and by degrees the knowledge of the things which I had seen increased within me,' and he sees 'a Figure sat upon a Throne, neither Man nor Woman, but Humanity in the Womb of Time – the Ellipse of the Absolute...Then my soul grew bewildered with the beauty of that face, and I covered myself with my hands, and when again I opened my eyes I felt the breath of dawn upon my face, and I heard the lark singing above, and the joy of calm was in my heart, and the morning star shone in all its glory above the Solitude of the Desert.'[22]

Occult author Manly P. Hall, in his essay *The Tarot*, written in the early twentieth century, showed that he had got wind of the Sufi and, perhaps, the Mesopotamian connections:

'There is a persistent rumour that the Tarot cards formed an integral part of the symbolism of the Arabian Mysteries, especially the arcane doctrines of the dervishes. Although conclusive evidence is unavailable, it is reported that pictorial devices, arranged in the form of a deck of cards, were in circulation among the mysterious wise men of Fez and Damascus. It was among these elusive adepts that the equally elusive Father C. R. C. of Rosicrucian manifestoes is said to have been initiated.'

Hall's conclusion is that it was the Knights Templar who brought the cards back to Europe with them 'among the philosophical mysteries which (they) contacted among the old mystics of Syria and Arabia...The Templars are said to have brought these cards with them because they realized that all the knowledge of the ages was epitomized in this little loose-leaf picture book.'[23]

He also refers to the book *Tarot of the Bohemians* by 'Papus,' real name Gerard Encausse, who, like his more famous colleague in the nineteenth century French occult revival, L'Abbe Constant, or 'Eliphas Levi,' tried to apply the Tarot in all sorts of imaginative ways and in combination with the *sefirothic* tree, perhaps with some garbled inspiration from informed sources. One thing that can be said with some confidence is that the 'Tarot of the Bohemians' had to do with divining gypsies only by default, and that it was, in reality, 'The Tarot of the *Mohammedans.*'

In the discussion of The Wheel of Fortune the possibility was considered that it was originally intended as some sort of representation of or reference to the enneagram; and in considering the Kabbalah, with its components the *sefiroth*, it was noted that authoritative sources aver that the form of the Kabbalah we have inherited differs from the original in that the original version had eight, not ten, *sefiroth*.

The fourteenth century, Scholem notes, was the one in which the Kabbalah spread from Spain to Italy. Cards were popular enough in Germany in 1329 to be banned by the Church, and the Bembo/Visconti cards of 1422 are clearly Tarot. In view of what appears now to be their and the enneagram's identical deeper origin, it will not be unreasonable to seek correlations among them that may prove illuminating. The Kabbalah had eight *sefiroth*, and one of the 'laws' the enneagram is supposed to express is the 'law of seven,' or 'law of octaves.' The musical scale has seven notes, eight if you count both 'doh's – which involves or implies the notion of it as a dynamic and developing thing, just as the enneagram, a circle with nine points, is in motion, and part of its information concerns the relationship of any living thing, or 'cosmos,' with the world outside of it, nothing alive existing in isolation. One may then speculate whether a diagrammatic, geometric representation of eightness may be said to have some sort of instructive relationship with the diagram of the nine points, and whether, and if so how, one may be the unfolding of the other.

A story, 'Dividing Camels,' in Idries Shah's 1971 book *Thinkers of the East* may have some bearing on it. A Sufi wanted his three disciples to find the right teacher for them after he died, and left them seventeen camels, instructing them to divide them up in such a way that the oldest had half, the middle one had a third, and the youngest had one-ninth. After much trial and error they found Ali, son in law of Mohammed, who solved the problem by adding one camel, bringing the total to eighteen, and making the divisions according to the teacher's instructions possible. The one camel left over returned to Ali himself.

If the seventeen is taken as representing the nine of the living, breathing, moving reality in combination or juxtaposition with the eight of static representation of the same reality, with 'one'/'nine' 'hidden within' it, the story suggests that the 'one'/'nine' that has to be added, or revealed, in order to bring it all to life is, from one point of view, the mind of the percipient himself. The nineness of the enneagram corresponds to the eternally alive and fluxing nature of both metaphysical reality and right brain mentation, in which the 'I' that is separated off in left brain mentation becomes 'part of the process.'

Then again, the three disciples may allude to the forces of the law of three. Arabic for 'nine' (the number of camels for the first disciple) is *tis'a*, and for 'six' (for the second disciple), *sitta*. Consonantally, they are like mirror images of each other. 'Two,' the number of camels the third disciple gets, is *ithnan*: *ta'ana* means 'to battle each other,' as the (so-called) positive and negative forces of the first two components of the law of three forces do. In the context of what is said about the workings of the law of three, the outcome of the 'battle' between the first and second forces is itself the third force: *tawwan* (after *ithnan* again) means 'immediately, right now, this very moment,' suggesting a breaking-through into the realm of time, of phenomenality; 'three,' moreover, is *thalatha*, and *tallaw* is 'emerge, appear, show up.' The nine is also one, *wahid*; *hadd* means 'limit, extremity, termination point'; the nineness of the nine camels the first disciple receives is one end of the process, and the one-ninth of the total the third disciple gets is, one might say, the other end of it; but these are the concrete phenomenal results, within the context of the 'eight' world, the left-brain world, in which both the sublime origin and the participation of the subjective 'I' are, or at least are considered to be, absent. From the point of view of the totality, the nine the first disciple receives is one-half, partaking of twoness, which is another way of saying the beginning of division is the end of wholeness, of the one.

The teaching about the law of octaves says that when the intervals are not filled by consciously reinforcing energy, the process changes direction, and eventually becomes the opposite of what it started out as. If we apply this to the first two forces in the law of three, that means that the second, 'denying' force is itself the result of the first force so extended: another meaning of the 'twoness' of *ithnan* is *thani*, 'turn away, deflect.' When it manifests in what we think of as reality, it has become the third force, and further sound-associations with *thalatha* include 'something, anything.'

On the 'return journey,' the arrangement of the forces would, one thinks, be different: one word that sounds like 'six' in Arabic (the number of camels received by the second disciple, who may represent the denying force in a descending octave, but something else in reverse: the 'repairing' of the deflections) means 'separate, disperse,' but a different one means 'mix together.'

It would seem, in other words, that there are, at the very least, grounds for thinking that these ideas are woven right into the Arabic language itself.

Gurdjieff, as reported by Ouspensky, famously confirmed that the enneagram as he had divulged it was incomplete and, in particular, that it was not possible, using only the material he had given, to connect it with a comprehensive representation of the law of seven, and that the means to do so were more complicated than he had shown.

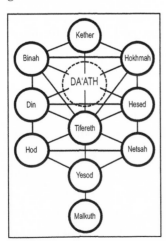

The ten *sefiroth* in their traditional arrangement are shown in Figure 66.

In addition to what is shown here, *En Sof*, or *Ein Sof*, the 'absolutely infinite,' is sometimes included, usually above *Kether*, 'crown,' as its source and the source of all the *sefiroth*. Some authors have maintained that the *Ein Sof* and *Kether* are distinct, others that they are, at least in some sense, the same.

Figure 66. Kabbalistic *sefirothic* tree.

Likewise, *Da'ath*, or 'knowledge,' is sometimes added – with the word, enclosed by a circle or a broken circle to indicate its fluid and ubiquitous nature with respect to the *sefiroth*, in the upper middle among them, between *Kether* and *Tifereth*. Leo Schaya, in *The Universal Meaning of the Kabbalah*, maintains that the positioning thus of *Da'ath* alludes to God's omniscience and omnipresence, so that *Da'ath* is not itself a *sefirah* but, rather, the knowing presence of the divine in each *sefirah*. Even so, the idea of God's omniscience itself came to be seen by Kabbalists as corresponding to the blending of the upper *sefiroth Hokmah* and *Binah*, which would be the knowledge that the divine singularity has of the whole of creation, as distinct from its knowledge of itself (the latter of which would be the meaning of *Hokmah* alone).

Two facts need to be borne in mind: that there is, in Kabbalistic lore, in addition to the ten *sefiroth*, an element above and outside them that represents 'the infinite,' and another one within them that has been translated as 'knowledge,' but an Arabic homonym of which, *dhat*, means 'essence,' which is significant in Sufi teaching.

Regarding the *Ein Sof*, the 'absolutely infinite,' such a formulation is easily comparable in its meaning with the being-beyond-being from which all originates in the Sufi metaphysical scheme already looked at; it also sounds rather like something approximating 'eye of purity' in Arabic, and one may speculate whether, as we have seen happened so often, a meaning on one level – in this case, that of perception through the part of oneself that can be relatively free from conditioned influences – has been lost, and its terminology applied to another.

The Arabic phrase *adh dhat 'ain as sifa* appears in the *Insan al Kamil* of Abd al Karim al Jili. *Sifa* means 'attributes,' and the phrase is a reference to the metaphysical viewpoint, to which Jili adhered, that the attributes of something are really the same as the thing's essence. Although the Arabic definite article is *al* (or *el*), when it appears before a word beginning with a consonant like the *sad* in *sifa*, the *lam* is not pronounced, so that *'ain as sifa* sounds almost exactly the same as *Ein Sof*. Scholem says that the term *Ein Sof* was first used in Isaac the Blind's commentary on the *Sefer Yetzirah*, which appeared in 1130 CE. Jili flourished in the late fourteenth and early fifteenth centuries CE, but the first known Sufi reference to an idea of a 'perfect and complete man' – *al kamil at tamm* – was by Abu Yazid al Bistami, 'Bayazid Bistami,' who is also on record as the first to articulate the concept of annihilation, *fana* (of the self), in God, which is conceptually strongly linked to the idea of the 'perfect man' as the microcosm through which God is conscious of Himself, which is in turn linked to the notion of the reality of (in this case, God's) attributes. Bistami died in 859 CE.

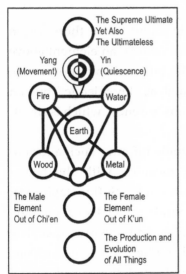

Figure 67. The T'ai Chi T'u of Chou Tun-I, or Diagram of the Supreme Ultimate[24]

It may be worth noting, too, that an apparently similar diagrammatic formulation existed in China and that, while it is frequently stated in contemporary Sufi literature that their knowledge has no origin in time and space, and is identical with all true wisdom-streams regardless of what form their local manifestation takes, the late poet Robert Graves, who is known, at least, to have assisted with the projection of Sufi teaching in the West in the past century, stated in a book of essays that was one of his last publications that it appears that Sufism began in China, and pointed to China's historical hegemony over Khorasan for corroboration.

Figure 67 shows a diagram from tenth century China. Ancient

Taoist thinkers strove to express the eternal interplay of the basic universal forces of yin and yang pictorially, and the result was a number of diagrams and charts like the one shown here. It was and is believed by some in that milieu that the Diagram of the Supreme Ultimate has its origin before recorded history.

While numerous variations on the basic idea of such a diagram were produced by different philosophers in China, with some of the elements of the diagram sometimes corresponding, for instance, to the five elements of Chinese thinking, the apparent extreme antiquity of its prototype, together with its striking visual resemblance to the Kabbalistic *sefirothic* tree, not to mention its very purpose, argue for our considering them in relation to each other. What is especially close is the presence at the top of the symbol representing 'the Ultimateless, yet the Supreme Ultimate'; and at the bottom, in the tree, *malkuth*, or 'kingdom,' representing the created world in which we live, and in the T'ai Chu T'u, the 'production and evolution of all things.' The Chinese diagram, moreover, includes (like the enneagram) movement inasmuch as it has the opposite but complementary elements of yin and yang, even if yin itself represents quiescence in contradistinction to yang's movement.

Unfortunately, it is not much more helpful in discerning the original version of the *sefirothic* tree, if only because it is difficult to see correspondences between the Chinese elements and the other *sefiroth*; but this may be as much a matter of our ignorance of one, if not of both, of them, as anything else. Nevertheless, the resemblance is interesting, especially in view of Graves' remark.

Further attention needs to be given to the correspondence between the *Da'ath* of the *sefirothic* tree, the *dhat* of the dervishes, and the inner triangle of the enneagram.

The idea that the essence of a thing is what makes it that thing, without which it would cease to be what it is – in the case of something living, presumably, this would correspond to, at least where physical existence is concerned, death – is potentially instructive when one considers that, in the enneagram, it is the function of the inner triangle (points 3, 6 and 9) to supply the 'shocks' or conscious filling-in-the-gaps at what correspond to the intervals that occur, as in the musical scale, in the course of the circulation of movement around and within the diagram. It is the filling of these intervals with new energy and impetus that prevents the natural tendency for the process in question (even where the process is a thing) to tend toward its own opposite: entropy, and also enables the octave, whatever it is in the given case, to maintain or regain a connection with its origin.

With the doing-away of the idea of the octave, with its intervals and their significance, the role of the *Da'ath* in the *sefirothic* tree is also susceptible to becoming a basis for arbitrary theorizing.

Is there anything else in Kabbalistic lore as we have received it that suggests the survival of the idea of a process, in time, in some sense cyclical, involving eight elements and a hierarchical ontology?

The late Gershom Scholem, undoubtedly the best known scholar of Kabbalah and Jewish mysticism of our time, wrote in his book *Origins of the Kabbalah* about the first group identifiable as a Kabbalistic one to appear in Spain (Gerona, a small town between Barcelona and the Pyrenee mountains) in the thirteenth century. Their location, he points out, situated them well for absorbing other esoteric traditions represented in the same general area at the time, and they would have incorporated them into their Kabbalism.

Teachings pertaining to cosmic cycles from sources in India and among the Arabs are known to have found homes in the thinking of medieval Jewish philosophers, but one doctrine in particular attained special importance in the Gerona school and, thus, for the development of the Kabbalah. The doctrine in question is that about the *shemittoth,* or 'world cycles,' and it was expressed in an anonymous work entitled *Temunah.* The *shemittoth* teaching held that God's power of creation is not confined to the *sefiroth*, and also encompasses their manifestation in creations that occur in sequence and succession. It is only possible for all that is hidden within the *sefiroth* to be completely exteriorized by its doing so through individual cosmic singularities each of which exists and functions in a way appropriate to the particular *sefirah* being expressed. It is at this point that the distinction between the upper three and the lower seven *sefiroth* becomes of practical significance. The upper three, *Kether*, *Hokmah* and *Binah*, are, as it were, in the *shemittoth* doctrine, inherent and concealed powers constituting three aspects of the fundamental informing capacity of the godhead and, unlike the lower seven, are not visibly (or at least obviously) active in the world, in the sense of being recognizable as stages in cosmic building processes. The other seven *sefiroth*, on the other hand, were held to directly correlate to the days of creation of the Genesis story; and each, in fact, constitutes a creation that is separate and self contained.

Scholem goes on to describe how, in the Gerona school, each of these latter was believed to last 7000 years, or one of God's weeks, with a period of fallowness between them, taking their cue from the Book of Deuteronomy.

Elsewhere he notes that the *shemittoth* teaching is perceptibly related to systems followed by non-Jewish sources the influence of which on Jewish thinkers is traceable in Spain and Muslim nations. Within the teaching, moreover, one of the appellations of the *sefirah Binah* is 'mother of the world.' Although Scholem does not mention it, 'mother of the world' is obviously similar to 'Mother of the Book,' one of the terms applied in the scheme of the *Ikhwan as Safa* to the Universal Intelligence, the first (and, from a certain point of view, the only) thing created by God.

It thus seems at least possible that the eight *sefiroth* of the original Kabbalah of the *Ikhwan as Safa* and the Sufis consisted of the seven lower *sefiroth* of the Kabbalah known to us, plus the three upper *sefiroth* combined into one; if so, it would confirm Blavatsky's assertion that the division of the top *sefirah* into three is a 'blind.' Moreover, the description of the first three *sefiroth* as 'hidden potencies' that 'do not act in the visible sphere' as do the other seven obviously closely parallels the relationship, and difference, between the law of three and the law of seven as Gurdjieff taught them.

On the other hand, this scheme still does not, on the face of it, correspond with the 'nine numbers of the 'Faithful Brothers,'' the *Ikhwan as Safa* – eight plus God, as it were – spoken of by the author of the *Jewish Encyclopedia* article.

The sequence of emanations, again, as he and others have transmitted them is as follows: 1. The creating spirit. 2. The directing spirit, or world soul. 3. Primal matter. 4. Active nature. 5. The abstract body, or secondary matter. 6. The world of the spheres. 7. The elements of the sublunary world. 8. The world of minerals, plants and animals.

The ten *sefiroth* of the Kabbalistic 'tree' are traditionally given, with minor variations in transliteration, as follows: 1. *Kether*, 'Crown.' 2. *Hokmah*, 'Wisdom.' 3. *Binah*, 'Intelligence.' 4. *Hesed*, 'Grace' or 'Love.' 5. *Din*, 'Severe Judgment,' or, sometimes, *Gevurah*, 'Power.' 6. *Rahamim*, 'Compassion,' or, sometimes, *Tifereth*, 'Beauty.' 7. *Netsah*, 'Victory.' 8. *Hod*, 'Majesty' or 'Glory.' 9. *Yesod*, 'Foundation.' 10. *Malkuth*, 'Kingdom.'

Some of these terms (also shown in Figure 68) correspond directly with Arabic words that occur frequently in Sufi metaphysical writing. *Hikmat* means 'wisdom,' especially 'divine wisdom'; *din* ('deen') means 'judgment, victory,' and also 'religion, faith'; *rahim*, of course, means 'mercy' or 'compassion'; *jabarut* means 'power,' especially 'spiritual power'; and *malakut* means 'kingdom,' from *malik*, 'king.' Others, by their sound, correspond directly with Arabic words the meaning of which is not, however, the meaning assigned to them in Hebrew in the *sefirothic* 'tree': but is, on the other hand, the meaning – and

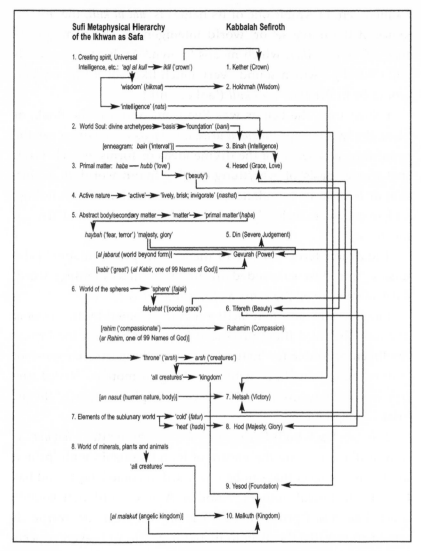

Figure 68

sometimes the meaning in an unexpected way – of some other term in the same scheme.

Assuming that the sequence and terms given as those of the *Ikhwan* are correct, the first one, the 'creating spirit,' corresponds with the Primal Intelligence, the Reality of Mohammed, the

Exalted Pen. In Arabic one of its names is *'aql al kull*, the 'intelligence of the universe' or 'world intelligence.' The name of the first *sefirah* is *Kether*, which means 'crown.' Arabic for 'crown' is *iklil* ('ikleel') – which sounds very much like *'aql al kull*, or, as it would be in Persian, *'aql i kull* ('aql ee kull').

Drawn from the Pen as was Eve from Adam is the Book, or Slate, the 'world soul,' *'alam al arwah*, the *nafs* of the universe, the repository, in a sense, of the divine ideas or forms or archetypes that are the 'basis' of everything existing in our world. In Arabic, *bani* or *baniyan* is 'foundation,' as in 'foundation of a building': and, of course, that closely resembles *Binah* in sound, and *Yesod* in meaning.

The Arabic term – or one of them – for 'primal matter,' *haba*, means 'fine dust suspended in air.' A similar-sounding word, *hubb*, means 'love,' the same as the *sefirah Hesed*.

Ibn al 'Arabi says that 'active nature,' created by the *'alam al arwah*, is the third thing produced in sequence from the Primal Intelligence. Arabic for 'nature' is *tabiyat*; the particular sense of 'nature' here, though, is 'active,' 'setting in motion.' *Nashat* (the *sefirah Netsah*) means, literally, 'drive from place to place,' 'lively, brisk,' 'invigorate.'

The 'abstract body,' *jism*, or 'secondary matter,' *hayula*, is 'physical' matter, and the nature of its relationship with 'primal matter' is a subject that can be discussed at some length, and has been by historical authors. Another Arabic word that sounds much like *haba* ('primal matter') is *haybah*: 'fear' or 'terror.' It would appear that the dichotomy of the gentle and severe aspects of divinity – *jamal*, 'beauty,' and *jalal*, 'majesty,' for instance – have here been applied, or misapplied, with each being assigned to one of the two kinds of 'matter.' The gradations of being in this scheme of the *Ikhwan* do not represent aspects of divinity, but stages of manifestation. Nor do they, as given, have intricate and specific interconnections as seen in the *sefirothic* 'tree.' The intermittent inclusion in the midst of the latter of *Da'ath*, 'knowledge,' however, and the interconnections of the points of the circum-ference of the enneagram, the inner triangle of which is supposed to represent the vital status of the thing or process represented, does suggest that the formulators of the *sefirothic* Kabbalah were trying to produce something of their own by combining elements of the teaching of the *Ikhwan* and the enneagram of the Sarmoun, and other Sufi doctrines as well. In the case of 'secondary matter,' it has been taken, as it were by default, to be the 'glorious' or 'majestic' aspect of divine reality that has been further confused with the 'fear' or 'terror' that it (or something else) might arouse in an individual, which is what *haybah* means.

Similarly, the range of meanings associated with 'majesty' probably produced the 'severity' of the 'severe judgment' that is the meaning of the *sefirah Din*.

'Sphere,' as in 'world of the spheres,' the next emanation after 'secondary matter,' in Arabic is *falak*. *Falqaha(t)* means 'grace' (the meaning of the *sefirah Hesed* or, perhaps, that of *Tifereth*) in the sense of 'polite manners, social graces.' Undoubtedly another kind or level of 'grace' altogether was intended by *Hesed*, but the term carried over. Another name for this level of being is 'throne,' *'arsh*.

The elements of the sublunary world: it is these that are said to have been divided into two by the Kabbalists. There are four: heat, cold, moisture and dryness; or, fire, air, water and earth. Again, the sense of 'heat' and 'cold' has been overlooked, so that *hada(t)*, 'heat' in the sense of an individual's temperament of being inclined to activity or violence, has given us the *sefirah Hod*. *Fatur*, 'cold' in the sense of 'lukewarm, indifferent,' may well have been compounded with *furutat*, 'sweet' (if, extending the tree analogy, the essence, *dhat*, or 'sap' of the 'tree' may be said to be 'sweet'), to produce the name *Tifereth*.

'Arsh means 'throne,' but a closely similar word, *arsh*, in Arabic means 'creatures,' in the sense of 'all creatures.' In its

meaning it corresponds with the *sefirah Malkuth*, 'kingdom', even though in the *Ikhwan*'s formulation it was meant to comprise 'minerals, plants, and animals,' but not humans.

Bain or *baun* (*Binah*) means 'interval' or 'interstice,' which is of interest if the enneagram was referred to, because of the intervals in the 'law of octaves.'

Gevurah, or *Geburah*, could also come from *kabir*, as in *al insan al kabir*, 'the big man' (the macrocosm). *Netsah*, the *sefirah*, may mean 'victory,' but it also, in addition to *nashat*, sounds a good deal like *nats*, 'intelligent, clever' (the meaning of the *sefirah Binah*), and also *nasut*, 'humanity,' which, like *jabarut*, is the name of one of the five broad hierarchical divisions: *al hahut* (God's essential nature), *al lahut* (divine creative nature), *al jabarut* (world beyond form, divine power), *al malakut* (angelic kingdom) and *an nasut* (human nature and body).

There have always been at least two schools of thought regarding the origin of the Kabbalah, even where it has been assumed to be an undistorted and, as it were, pure product. Modern scholarship, as far as it has gone, has tended in favor of a medieval formulation; but there have always been those with a strong commitment to its extreme antiquity, who have said it antedates all recorded religious manifestations. If the demonstration of its derivation from a wisdom tradition that does, in fact, fit that description isn't enough for them, perhaps further evidence of the presence of that knowledge, which is also – as has been seen – as modern as can be imagined in that most ubiquitous of sources, the Hebrew Bible, what Christians call the Old Testament, will be.

There is even a further irony inasmuch as it is one place where hints may be found of how items as seemingly disparate as the law of seven and the dual nature of human consciousness, as well as other things, may be harmonized.

The second Book of Samuel contains a number of stories: among them, in the second chapter, stories of the strife between

Abner, who had been the general of the now deceased King Saul, and who made Saul's son Ishbosheth King of Israel in Mahanaim, on one side of the Jordan River, and David, King of the tribe of Judah in Hebron, on the other side.

The narrative relates how Abner and Ishbosheth's soldiers one day just happened to run into Joab with David's soldiers 'at the pool in Gibeon.' They sat down on opposite sides of the pool, and Abner suggested that they have their best soldiers engage in combat. Twelve of Ishbosheth's best Benjaminites and twelve of David's prime crew, it says, 'grabbed each other by the hair and stabbed each other in the side with their daggers. They all died right there!...Then everyone started fighting. Both sides fought very hard, but David's soldiers defeated Abner and the soldiers of Israel.'

The status of the combatants as 'the best' is a clue that it is something as relatively elusive as qualities that are being discussed. The law of three has it that where there is no third, reconciling or neutralizing force, the first two forces, the positive and negative, though they may meet, can, by themselves, produce nothing: just as the twelve warriors on each side exactly match, and then perfectly annihilate, each other. A pool, too, is a stagnant body of accumulated water: Arabic words for it emphasize that aspect, of coming together, collection, combination. The rest of the soldiers then join the fray, and the victors, David's surviving men, may be said to represent the produced-with-difficulty third force.

David is not actually present; his men are, as mentioned, led by Joab, who is 'the son of Zeruiah'. 'Zeruiah's three sons were there,' it continues, 'Joab, Abishai and Asahel. Asahel could run as fast as a deer in an open field, and he ran straight after Abner, without looking to the right or to the left.' These characteristics of Asahel reveal him as representing the activity of the left hemisphere of the brain, the analytic function, which knows only its target, its goal to be achieved, and which is impatient with anything not devoted to the same purpose. In the context, as it will be seen, although it says all three sons 'were there,' Abishai remains behind: he is thus the passive force. Joab represents the reconciling force, and in the interplay of these things is to be seen the story within the story.

As has been noted, it is said in the lore about the law of seven and the enneagram that where an interval in the octave occurs, if the process the octave represents is to proceed with undiminished force or without misdirection, the gap of the interval must be filled by energy from the source of the process itself or, hypothetically, from some other, coincidental, source. From a certain point of view, of course, all processes and all energies ultimately have the same source anyway. To that extent, then, the resulting third force – that enables the process to get past its stage of self bafflement, the state of mutual thwarting of the opposed 'affirming' and 'denying' forces – and the undifferentiated origin are one and the same. Perception of difference, as noted previously, is the domain of the left brain. The role of the right brain has also been touched on, how it is concerned with simultaneity, spatiality, and wholeness, in what has traditionally been called 'mystical' experience, which is generally taken to mean man's and woman's experience of wholes, of comprehensive realities, from which humanity is customarily separated, or at least feels itself to be because of the imbalance that has existed throughout recorded human history as a result of the over-emphasis on left brain-type thinking.

There is thus no contradiction in saying that Asahel represents both the activity of the left brain and the active force in the law of three, bearing in mind that in any real context the definitions of these things are relative.

So he goes running after Abner. If it is taken that the point of the allegory is to tell us something useful in the context of improving our understanding of these matters, it does not seem too much of a stretch to say that Abner probably represents the knowledge itself that we are seeking: which is just like the Hermit in the Tarot cards – knowledge seeking the seeker, whatever it may look like he is doing.

Abner turns and sees Asahel, and says, "Is that you, Asahel?"

Are you separate, Asahel? Do you know 'who you are', that you are not me, not anyone else – that you are you, only you?

"Yes it is."

Abner then says to him: "There are soldiers all around. Stop chasing me and fight one of them! Kill him and take his clothes and weapons for yourself."

What you are looking for, what you need, is to be found all around you. You are not really separate. It's the very thing you are doing to get what you want that stops you getting what you want.

'But Asahel refused to stop.'

Abner then threatens to kill him if he doesn't 'turn back,' adding, "Then I could never face your brother Joab again."

Which is very interesting, because Joab and Abner are on opposite sides, their armies trying to kill each other. Why should he even want to 'face him' again? How can that which has one face, face itself?

'But Asahel would not turn back, so Abner struck him in the stomach with the back end of his spear. The spear went all the way through and came out of his back. Asahel fell down and died.'

The front end of a spear is the sharp, fine end. The back end is the blunt, clumsy end. Asahel has run smack into his own nature, and his nature is to be limited: to have an end.

'Everyone who saw Asahel lying dead just stopped and stood still.'

The first interval.

Joab (*jaub*, 'traversing, exploring (foreign lands); piercing, penetrating'; 'to answer, reply; to comply with; to be mutually corresponding, harmonize'; 'to pay attention, show interest';

jawab, 'answer; octave') and Abishai (*bas'a*, 'to be intimate, be on familiar terms with'; *bash*, 'smiling, happy, friendly, kind'; *basis*, 'glow, shine'; *bassa*, embers; *bassas*, 'spy, detective'), who up to this point have not moved (which makes little sense if taken literally) then continue the chase: the third force energy, from 'the source,' fills the gap. The removal of Asahel also means the changing of Abishai's significance as representing the passive force. His accompanying Joab may be taken to indicate a previously unused potential: perhaps the potential of everything the left brain keeps in check.

'Finally, about sunset, they came to the hill of Ammah, not far from Giah on the road to Gibeon Desert.' Abner gathers his men, of the tribe of Benjamin, on a hill. He shouts to Joab, "Aren't we ever going to stop killing each other? Don't you know that the longer we keep on doing this, the worse it's going to be when it's all over? When are you going to order your men to stop chasing your own relatives?'

'Joab shouted back, 'I swear by the living God, if you hadn't spoken, my men would have chased their relatives all night!' Joab took his trumpet and blew the signal for his soldiers to stop chasing the soldiers of Israel. Right away, the fighting stopped.

'Abner and his troops marched through the Jordan River valley all that night. Then they crossed the river and marched all morning until they arrived back at Mahanaim.'

The second interval ('right away, the fighting stopped') is filled by the understanding of which Asahel (*sahula*, 'to deem easy, think to be easy'; *shahula*, 'to accelerate, speed up') was incapable, the realization of the shared reality ('your own relatives') that, ultimately, is not only a matter of chasing and of taking, but also of allowing to be given.

The story of the rebellion of 'Sheba the son of Bichri' (Second Samuel, Chapter 20) offers startlingly vivid further evidence of the presence in the Hebrew religious writings of the knowledge of what have come to be called in our time the law of seven and the law of three, and also, perhaps, of how they are to be understood in relation to other subjects such as the polarity inherent in human consciousness, involving the opposite tendencies to crudity and subtlety, to calculation and experience of the whole, to self seeking and a relationship with reality beyond the self that has more in common with things like humility and service.

The figure of Sheba (*sabi'a*, 'abuse, insults'), a 'troublemaker from the tribe of Benjamin' who 'blew a trumpet to get everyone's attention' and, once he had got it, convinced the Israelites that "David the son of Jesse doesn't belong to us," and that they should follow him instead, stands in direct contrast to the one in the immediately preceding chapter of Barzillai, an eighty-year-old who 'was very rich and had sent food to David in Mahanaim.' David invites Barzillai to cross the Jordan River with him on his way to reclaiming the throne in Jerusalem, but Barzillai (*bari zalla*, 'without error'; *barra*, 'charitable, dutiful, reverent,' *zalla*, 'continue, persevere'; *bar*, 'creation', *zawal*, 'end, extinction, disappearance') replies that there would really not be much point in view of the fact that his age means he doesn't have long to live: "My body is almost numb. I can't taste my food or hear the sound of singing...I'll cross the river with you, but I'll only go a little way on the other side...Just let me return to my hometown, where I can someday be buried near my father and mother.'

He offers David his servant, 'Chimham,' to go with him as his own, which he does. Barzillai goes home. 'All of Judah's army and half of Israel's army' are there to help David make the crossing and, when it is accomplished, the Israelite soldiers complain about what they see as the sneakiness of David's Judean relatives in their manner of assistance, to which the Judeans reply by querying the Israelites on their anger, and by pointing out that they, the Judeans, are related to David, and that they had taken no food for themselves from the king.

The soldiers of Israel assert that David "belongs to us ten times more than he belongs to you," and complain that the

Judeans obviously have a low opinion of them, even though they, the Israelites, had the idea of bringing David back first. Yet, curiously, the chapter concludes by saying that 'the people of Judah spoke more harshly than the people of Israel.'

Barzillai's characteristics identify him as representing the same spiritual reality as is signified by the figures of Esau and Enkidu. He is an old man (*himm*) full of concern (*hamm*) for David. His senses have all but completely faded; his grip on the physical realm is very tenuous. That reality itself cannot 'cross over' into the other, cruder one, but it can 'send' 'Chimham' – *jam* (concentration of one's thoughts) *himma* (high aspiration) – to go with the individual as he makes his or her way through the world. *Jama'a*, moreover, includes meanings of 'meeting, gathering, integrating' (as the Judeans and the Israelites did), and *hami'a* means 'be or become angry.'

Sheba is the opposite of what is represented by Barzillai. He makes a great deal of sound and fury to the purpose of diverting all from following the true king, inducing them to follow him instead.

The twentieth chapter, then, superficially describes David's strategy for dealing with Sheba, who has taken 'the people of Israel' with him. He orders Amasa to muster Judah's army in three days. Amasa sets about it, but he misses the deadline. David then tells Abishai to 'take my best soldiers and go after' Sheba. Abishai takes with him 'Joab and his soldiers, as well as David's bodyguard and best troops.'

In Gibeon, Amasa catches up with them. 'Joab had a dagger strapped around his waist over his military uniform, but it fell out as he started toward Amasa.'

What follows asks us to believe that Joab then greeted Amasa warmly, grasping Amasa's beard with his right hand (in the custom of the time and place, no doubt) in order the better to kiss him. Amasa doesn't see the dagger – the King James version calls it a 'sword' – in Joab's other hand, with the result that it pierces

Amasa's stomach (the King James says 'he smote him therewith in the fifth rib'), just once, so that Amasa's guts tumble out onto the ground. It says that the dagger or sword 'fell out,' but then seems to represent Joab as doing the deed of stabbing Amasa with it actively and with awareness.

Joab and Abishai then take off after Sheba.

Poor Amasa rolls around in his blood 'in the middle of the road,' while one of Joab's men stands there directing anyone who happens to come along to follow Joab if they approve of him and if they support David. He notices that, much as is the case with highway vehicle accidents in our time, passersby were stopping to take in the sight of Amasa in his agony, his insides now very much on the outside. The soldier, therefore, drags Amasa off the road 'into the field,' and covers him with a blanket or cloth. 'After this, no one else stopped. They all walked straight past him on their way to help Joab capture Sheba.'

Amasa (*masha*, 'to move along, proceed'; 'to adapt, adjust, fit'; 'to keep pace, keep in step'; 'to be guided by the same consider-ations or principles'; *mash*, 'tangent'; 'touching'; 'adjacent, adjoining, contiguous'; 'urgent, pressing, important'), of course, corresponds to the law of three (he is to gather the army in three days), which operates outside of time (his failure to meet the deadline for gathering them). In its relationship to the exteriorly-oriented, sequential and time-based nature of the law of seven, his nature is interior and hidden: his innards that are spilled. The forces of the law of three interact with and influence processes in time, which follow the law of seven and are subject to its intervals, or 'stopping places,' by having the effect of occupying or filling those intervals, enabling the process to continue. The precise and peculiar details of that interaction, the 'falling' of Joab's dagger and Joab's somehow-accidentally-or-maybe-not stabbing Amasa with it, delineate the interaction of relatively unconscious and mechanical reality with the more-conscious, less mechanical one.

References

1. H. P. Blavatsky. *Collected Writings: Miscellaneous (Vol. XIV)*. 1985 Theosophical Publishing House, Wheaton, Illinois. 106.
2. *Ibid*. 94.
3. *Ibid*. 174.
4. Shah Waliyullah. *Al-Khair al-Kathir*. Rendered into English by G. N. Jalbani. 1974 Ashraf, Lahore.
5. *Ibid*. 10.
6. *Ibid*. 18-9.
7. *Ibid*. 20-1
8. C. G. Jung. *Psychological Reflections*. Selected and edited by Jolande Jacobi. 1979 Routledge & Kegan Paul, London. 266.
9. Fulcanelli. *Le Mystere des Cathedrales*. Translated from the French by Mary Sworder. 1984 Brotherhood of Life, Albuquerque, New Mexico. 42.
10. T. P. Hughes. *A Dictionary of Islam*. No date. Premier Book House, Lahore. 181.
11. John A. Subhan. *Sufism, Its Saints and Shrines*. 1970 Samuel Weiser, New York. 55-6.
12. John P. Brown. *The Darvishes or Oriental Spiritualism*. 1968 Frank Cass, London. 153-54.
13. Waliyullah. *Op. cit*. 10.
14. Subhan. *Op. cit*. 231-32.
15. *The Jewish Encyclopedia: A Descriptive Record of the History, Religion, Literature, and Customs of the Jewish People from the Earliest Times. Vol. III. Bencemero-Chazamuth*. No date. (Preface dated 1901.) Ktav Publishing House, New York. 463-4.
16. H. P. Blavatsky. *Collected Writings. Vol. X*. 1964 Theosophical Publishing House, Adyar, Madras. 245.
17. *Jewish Encyclopedia. Op. cit*. 466.
18. Hughes. *Op. cit*. 84.
19. Muhammad Bin Khavendshah Bin Mahmud ('Mirkhond'). *The Rauzat-us-Safa, or, Garden of Purity, Containing the*

Histories of Prophets, Kings, and Khalifs. Part I. Volume First. Translated from the Original Persian by E. Rehatsek, edited by F. F. Arbuthnot. Oriental Translation Fund. New Series. 1891 Royal Asiatic Society, London. 75-8.

20. Brown. *Op. cit.* 202-03.
21. Mary Anne Atwood. *A Suggestive Inquiry into the Hermetic Mystery, With a Dissertation on the More Celebrated of the Alchemical Philosophers, Being an Attempt Towards the Recovery of the Ancient Experiment of Nature.* No date. (Reprint of 1918 edition.) Yogi Publication Society. No address.
22. Fairfax L. Cartwright. *The Mystic Rose From the Garden of the King. A Fragment of the Vision of Sheikh Haji Ibrahim of Kerbela.* 1976 Watkins, London.
23. Manly P. Hall. *The Tarot.* 1978 The Philosophical Research Society, Los Angeles. 1, 5, 6.

Sources

A. E. Affifi. *The Mystical Philosophy of Muhyid Din Ibnul Arabi*. 1964 Ashraf, Lahore.

Aflaki. *Munaqib al Arifin*. Various translations (e.g., Redhouse, Shah).

Khwaja Nazeer Ahmad. *Jesus in Heaven on Earth*. 1972 The Woking Muslim Mission and Literary Trust, The Mosque, Woking, England, and Azeez Manzil, Brandreth Road, Lahore.

Attar. *Tadhkirat al Awliya*. Multiple translations available. Quotations and references assisted especially by the translation by: Bankey Behari. *Selections from Fariduddin 'Attar's Tadhkaratul-Auliya or Memoirs of Saints Parts I & II*. 1975 Ashraf, Lahore.

J. G. Bennett. *Gurdjieff: Making a New World*. 1973 Turnstone, London.

All Biblical quotations from: *Holy Bible (Contemporary English Version)*. 1995 American Bible Society, New York.

Dominique Collon. *First Impressions: Cylinder Seals in the Ancient Near East*. 1988 University of Chicago Press.

Henry Corbin. *Cyclical Time and Ismaili Gnosis*. 1983 Kegan Paul International in association with Islamic Publications, London.

Da Liu. *T'ai Chi Ch'uan and Meditation*. 1987 Routledge & Kegan Paul 26. (Diagram from Fung Yu-Lan, *A History of Chinese Philosophy*, Vol. 2. 1953 Princeton University Press.)

Stephanie Dalley. *Myths from Mesopotamia: Creation, The Flood, Gilgamesh and Others*. OUP 1991.

Encyclopedia of World Mythology. Foreword by Rex Warner. 1975 Peerage, London.

Ghazali. *Ihya 'Alam ad Din*. All quotations and other references reworked from the English translation by: Alhaj Maulana Fazlul Karim. *Gazzali's Ihya Ulum-id-Din or Revival of Religious Learnings*. 1971 F. K. Islam Mission, Dacca, East Pakistan.

Robert Graves. 'The Sufic Chequer-Board,' in *Difficult Questions, Easy Answers*. 1972 Cassell, London.

John Gray. *Near Eastern Mythology*. 1975 Hamlyn, London.

Jacquetta Hawkes. *The First Great Civilizations*. 1973 Hutchinson, London.

Hujwiri. *Kashf al Mahjub*. Translated by R. A. Nicholson. 1970 Luzac, London.

Husaini, Moulvi S. A. Q. *Ibn al-'Arabi: The Great Muslim Mystic and Thinker*. 1970 Ashraf, Lahore.

Ibn 'Arabi. *Sufis of Andalusia. (The Ruh al-Quds and al-Durrat al-Fakhira*, Translated with Introduction and Notes by R. W. J. Austin.) 1971 George Allen & Unwin, London.

The Kabbalah Unveiled. Translated by S. L. MacGregor Mathers from the Latin 'Kabbala Denudata'. 1981 Routledge & Kegan Paul, London.

Khaja Khan. *Studies in Tasawwuf*. 1973 Ashraf, Lahore.

Khan Sahib Khaja Khan. *The Secret of Ana'l-Haqq. (Being 300 Odd Irshadat (or Sayings) of Shaykh Ibrahim Gazur-i-Ilahi*, Translated from the Persian with Notes and Introduction by Khan Sahib Khaja Khan.) 1971 Ashraf, Lahore.

All Koranic quotations from: *The Holy Qur'an*. Text, translation and commentary by A. Yusuf Ali. 1975 The Islamic Foundation, Leicester, U.K. in cooperation with The Muslim Students' Association of the United States & Canada.

Larousse World Mythology. Edited by Pierre Grimal. 1981 Hamlyn, London.

Seton Lloyd. *The Archaeology of Mesopotamia*. 1978 Thames & Hudson, London.

New Encyclopaedia Britannica. Vol. 2. Micropaedia. Ready Reference. 15th edition. 1992 Encyclopaedia Britannica, Inc.

Nicholson, R. A. *Studies in Islamic Mysticism*. 1978 CUP, Cambridge and London.

Joan Oates. *Babylon*. 1979 Thames & Hudson, London.

P. D. Ouspensky. *In Search of the Miraculous*. Various editions.

Rumi. *Discourses of Rumi*. Translated by A. J. Arberry. 1975 John Murray, London.

Rumi. *Selected Poems from the Divani Shamsi Tabriz*. Translated and edited by R. A. Nicholson. 1977 Cambridge University Press, Cambridge.

Shahab ad din Sahrawardi. *'Awarif al Ma'arif*. (Multiple translations and editions.)

The Rev. W. St. Clair-Tisdall. *The Sources of Islam*. Translated and abridged by Sir William Muir. 1980 Amarko Book Agency, New Delhi.

S. A. Salik. *The Saint of Jilan*. 1974 Ashraf, Lahore.

Sanai. *Hadiqat al Haqiqat*. All quotations reworked from the original Persian and the English translation by: Major J. Stephenson. *The First Book of the Hadiqatu'l-Haqiqat or the Enclosed Garden of the Truth of the Hakim Abu'l-Majdud Sana'i of Ghazna*. 1975 Thorsons, Wellingborough, England.

Leo Schaya. *The Universal Meaning of the Kabbalah*. Translated from the French by Nancy Pearson. 1973 Penguin, Baltimore.

Gershom G. Scholem. *Major Trends in Jewish Mysticism*. 1972 Schocken, New York.

Gershom Scholem. *Kabbalah*. 1978 Meridian, New York.

Gershom Scholem. *Origins of the Kabbalah*. Edited by R. J. Zwi Werblowsky and translated from the German by Allan Arkush. 1987 The Jewish Publication Society and Princeton University Press.

Idries Shah. *The Sufis*. 1971 Anchor/Doubleday, New York.

Idries Shah. *Thinkers of the East*. 1977 Octagon, London.

Shah Waliyullah. *Al-Khair al-Kathir*. Rendered into English by G. N. Jalbani. 1974 Ashraf, Lahore.

Kenneth Walker. *A Study of Gurdjieff's Teaching*. 1957 Jonathan Cape, London.

Roy G. Willis. *World Mythology*. 1993 Henry Holt, New York.

Diane Wolkstein and Samuel Noah Kramer. *Inanna, Queen of Heaven and Earth*. 1983 Harper & Row, New York.

BOOKS

O is a symbol of the world, of oneness and unity. In different cultures it also means the "eye," symbolizing knowledge and insight. We aim to publish books that are accessible, constructive and that challenge accepted opinion, both that of academia and the "moral majority."

Our books are available in all good English language bookstores worldwide. If you don't see the book on the shelves ask the bookstore to order it for you, quoting the ISBN number and title. Alternatively you can order online (all major online retail sites carry our titles) or contact the distributor in the relevant country, listed on the copyright page.

See our website **www.o-books.net** for a full list of over 500 titles, growing by 100 a year.

And tune in to myspiritradio.com for our book review radio show, hosted by June-Elleni Laine, where you can listen to the authors discussing their books.

mySpiritRadio